DANCING IN THE FALL

DANCING IN THE FALL

Embracing Joy in the midst of Change

Linda Bryant

Dancing in the Fall

© 2019 by Linda Bryant

Published by Vantage Point Associates, Inc.

Hoffman Estates, IL 60192

ISBN-13: 978-1-7343126-0-7

DEDICATION

For Ron

For always encouraging me to be authentic. You are my
patient and steady cheerleader. I will always dance with you.

For Jordan, Debralyn, and Josh

For graciously accepting me as you grew roots and
developed your wings. Each of you continue to inspire me.

For Dad

For modeling how to see the truth and beauty in fall.

CONTENTS

INTRODUCTION 9

SHIFTING WINDS...13
MOMENTS OF TRUTH 17
ROUND AND AROUND 23
THAT'S A WRAP 27
PLAYING IT SAFE 31
WHOEVER 'SHE' IS 35
TRUE COLORS..41
BINDWEED, CHOKEBERRIES, LIES 45
THAWING?...49
CLEAN FLOORS AND POTATO CHIPS 53

I SURRENDER 61
YOU TOO? 65
BANGING MY HEAD..69
JUST THREE QUESTIONS...................................73
UNDER CONSTRUCTION.....................................79
BRAVE NUMBER EIGHT.......................................81
SONGBIRDS AND STUFF 85
CLEARING OUT OVERGROWTH 89
PRELUDES AND FUGUES 93
COMPLETELY TORN OUT.....................................99

FINDING PENNIES 105

DAY BY DAY BY DAY...111

SURPRISED BY JOY..115

THE HIGHWAY OR THE WOODS 119

UNFAMILIAR PATHS..123

SLOW IT DOWN 127

VAULT FRIENDS 133

YOU GOT THIS..139

BLUE SKIES 147

DANCING FEET...153

SPECIAL THANKS 161

RESOURCES..163

TO CONNECT..165

INTRODUCTION

Why don't I feel anything?

Why am I exhausted trying to control peoples' opinions of me?

Why am I terrified to fail?

Why do I constantly compare myself to others?

Most importantly, why was I afraid of truly being me?

Many of the answers to those questions were right outside my kitchen window and alongside my nearby forest preserve path.

Day after day, month after month, and most importantly, season after season. I simply had to bravely admit my childlike desire to be outside still mattered. And I'm so grateful I did. Noticing the subtle messages and changes in the four seasons opened my eyes to my very own life.

Saying it was the first step. Believing it came second. Courageously incorporating it changed everything.

Just when I couldn't silence the nagging soundtrack in my heart about the uncontrollable changes happening in my life, fall spoke clearly and honestly to me. That's because fall is all about displaying what's real. About letting go. About harvesting what was planted. About seeing what's really going on beneath the surface.

Leaves fluttering to the ground. Combines slicing through endless rows of ripened grain. Maple leaves displaying their vibrant golds, reds, and oranges. The changes in fall suggest a gentle 'I surrender.' A weird contrast between emptying and filling.

Truthfully, I am much more comfortable with control than surrender. With holding on instead of letting go. The tension is real. Because I didn't like the 'me' that bubbled up amidst that battle, I knew I had to do something. To ask hard questions and seek honest answers.

After admitting my life was metaphorically in the season of fall, my internal battle began to lessen. Just like the season of fall, I sought to embrace the changes in my life to challenge me to let go of who I thought I should be and what I expected my life to be. Only by doing that could I become who I truly am and embrace real joy in my life.

I've lived this way for over a decade and wish I hadn't waited so long. Life really feels better to live as the real me. There's only one of me (and only one of you) so doesn't it make sense to live authentically? After trying life both ways, I'd clearly rather live the hardest of days being me than living the best of days just skating across the surface of a fake life.

If you've read *The Velveteen Rabbit*, you may remember the little stuffed rabbit's brave journey to becoming real. As he watched the real rabbits dance and shout with glee, he knew he wanted that. Yet, he was stuck in a body that didn't move. Becoming real for the little rabbit didn't come easily. But it came.

Just as the little rabbit's story inspired me, I hope my story inspires you.

PART I

"I don't like dancing. I'd rather sit still!"

But all the while he was longing to dance, for a funny new tickly feeling ran through him, and he felt he would give anything in the world to be able to jump around as these rabbits did.

The Velveteen Rabbit

SHIFTING WINDS

Running ten miles had never felt so easy. My effortless breathing, strong legs, and occupied mind combined perfectly with the warmth of the sun. Even though I was only nearing my halfway turnaround point, I was fairly confident I could run indefinitely. Nothing beats mid-autumn weather. Running, and perhaps life itself, couldn't get any better than this.

I quickly calculated my time and realized I was on pace for a personal best for this route!

Then I turned around. Just like that everything changed.

Why hadn't I noticed the wind? Facing a legitimate 30 mph headwind made me wonder why I hadn't felt it thrusting me forward minutes earlier. I'd certainly missed the momentum today.

While I still felt great, I admitted that this could negatively impact my return home pace a bit.

Nagging thoughts kept poking through my veil of optimism. Was the wind at my back the reason why my run had felt so effortless? More sobering was wondering if the 'wind at my back' was the reason my life felt so easy.

My energy faded in direct proportion to the headwind strengthening. Still, I tried to silence my silly thoughts and tried to convince myself I'd be fine.

Wrong.

As the wind continued to pick up speed, my warm autumn sun simultaneously decided to hide behind thick, billowy, gray clouds. Apparently, those clouds had been forming over the past hour, but they'd been at my back. I hadn't noticed ominous weather shifts. I'd been oblivious. Unprepared.

Next, the plummeting temperatures really caught my attention.

Thirty mile per hour headwind. Grey clouds. Windchill. Here I thought that I was going out to run in lovely 60- degree fall weather but now found myself in completely different circumstances. The change was dramatic. No longer was I paying attention to my effortless breathing, strong legs, or optimistic mental state. My entire being was consumed with the painful conditions that now overwhelmed me as I tried to make my way back home.

I was so cold.

I found myself scouring the roadside ditches for plastic bags to cover my bare fingers as they grew increasingly numb each second. While I'd been foolish to not anticipate the weather change, I was smart enough to know that without protecting my fingers, they'd be at risk for frostbite before I reached home.

I found a strip of clear plastic lying along the path and wrapped it around each hand like a cast. While it kept the wind off, plastic wrap was a weak substitute for warm gloves. I had about an hour of my run left, and I already had lost feeling in my fingertips. I was unprepared, scared, and alone.

Please realize I was literally still running on the same trail. But in the opposite direction under completely different conditions. The return trip home seemed endless.

When my run was easy, I hadn't really noticed much except the winding blacktop path ahead of me. Now that my run was incredibly hard, all I could do was look at the nameless faces driving on the highway next to me. In the midst of my pain, I couldn't stop myself from comparing their apparent comfort to my plight. I soon looked for anyone else to blame for my freezing fingers and weary body. Deep inside I knew that this wasn't the first time those types of 'conversations' with myself showed up.

After what felt like an eternity, I finally made it to the security of my home. Within minutes, my tears begin to flow. While I felt extreme relief, I had to face the nasty reality of unwrapping the plastic from my fingers. I couldn't feel a thing, yet I trembled at the thought of sticking my frozen fingers underwater trickling out of the kitchen faucet. My fear of remaining numb competed with my fear of the thawing pain.

The battle glared right back at me as I watched the lukewarm water trickle off my stiff, red fingers. Enduring the pin-pricking sensations of thawing almost made me vomit.

As feeling returned, I gradually increased the water temperature. After my hands returned to normal, I no longer had to be hunched over my kitchen sink.

Ironically, the process of regaining feeling almost made me want to stay numb. I thought to myself that I NEVER EVER wanted to experience pain in my fingers like that again. I vowed to be prepared for any weather change, and for the most part, I have been. Those are choices within my control.

Too bad life doesn't mirror that reality. I couldn't put that run out of my mind because I knew deep down that fickle fall day mirrored my life more than I wanted to admit.

I was "fine" when the wind was at my back. When life felt easy and fun. When I falsely believed that I was the one in control.

But enter chilling cold and strong headwinds. Enter changes that I could not control. Enter emotions such as sadness or loneliness or fear. You'd find me on my hands and knees scouring the 'roadside' for the perfect 'plastic' to keep my heart from feeling. I'd gotten good at it too after thirty or so years of practice. My heart had gotten pretty attached to those layers of plastic.

I'd lived too long declaring that I was fine even when I wasn't.

That ugly lie wasn't working anymore. I didn't like the woman who emerged when change flooded over me. So, hunched over my internal 'kitchen sink', I acknowledged the choice I needed to make.

I could keep layering my heart with discarded plastic bags and push through the cold and the wind on my own. Or I could go through the painful and frightening process of thawing out my heart to feel the real emotions changes in my life would surface.

I was intimidated by either path.

Timidly I tiptoed toward what my frozen fingertips taught me. You see, after they thawed, they could do what they were made to do. I deeply believed after my heart thawed, it could also do what it was made to do. I was able to use them again.

I had some work to do, so I began to let what I noticed fall teaching me gently find its way through the protective layers of plastic wrap I'd accumulated throughout my life. My life depended on it.

MOMENTS OF TRUTH

There was a time, not that long ago, that I realized I was someone else living my life. I didn't quite recognize who I'd become.

I wasn't real.

I was still a little girl when I concluded my 'job' was to make sure everyone else was ok. Then I made sure I portrayed the same 'ok' right back at them. I falsely believed this was the quickest way to prevent an angry outburst or a lengthy period of silence. I assumed and wore my role very seriously, but I didn't anticipate it would turn into the lie that being ok was the best way to be. Nobody ever told me to do this, and nobody would have wanted me to do this. But it was the way my mind and heart worked as I was figuring out my role in this world.

I learned how to listen to other voices rather than using my own. I found myself agreeing with people who I thought were more important than myself just because I didn't know how to speak up for myself. Unless I had the stomach flu or bronchitis, I didn't want to admit that I needed anything. It started early.

During recess in first grade, I'd done the right thing and faithfully waited for my turn to jump rope outside of my tiny schoolhouse. Just as I was ready to hop in, a second grader loudly declared that because it was her birthday, she would be FIRST at EVERYTHING all day long. I cowered under her strength.

Not just that day, but for the remaining eleven years that we attended school together.

By the time I finished sixth grade, I stood head and shoulders above the rest of my classmates. Growing nine inches in one year held its own sort of trauma, but words from a very vocal woman in my church seared a lie into my identity.

"I'd never realized you were such a big girl," she declared in front of my entire Sunday school class. I wanted to hide. To cut off inches and pounds. Instead, I smiled and mumbled something inaudible as I backed away from her. She'd made her point, and even though I gave her words too much power, my body image was redefined that day.

My ability to indiscriminately internalize messages was well underway. Coupled with my desire to make others feel 'ok' while projecting that I was also 'ok', I headed straight to the roll of plastic wrap so I could keep from feeling the dissonance in my heart.

I'd given over much of my identity to the whims and words of others.

The impact accumulated like a growing thunderstorm, but I'd bought into the lie that I wasn't quite enough on the inside, so I needed to work just a little bit harder to prove my worth on the outside.

So, I did what I'd gotten very comfortable doing. Day by day, season by season, year by year, I worked harder and smiled bigger, and ignored the stranger living inside me. Even though I was growing wearier and more worried, less joyful and loving. Living behind a mask was exhausting as a teenager but living under a disguise with a husband and three children was almost impossible.

Here's the truth. My life had so much to celebrate! I was married to a godly and loving and attentive husband. Ron was a successful, busy executive in the marketplace and a respected elder in our church. His success brought financial security and opportunities to travel. We had three amazing children, and I had the privilege of homeschooling. Jordan, Debralyn, and Josh were thriving in ways unique to the way they were wired. We had a lovely home, freshly remodeled and redecorated. I had more than enough of pretty much anything anybody could ever want. But I was spending so much of my energy and focus holding any negative emotion under the surface that all I had left to display was that evil four-letter word - fine.

I'd figured out how to set up my entire life to portray the fact that I was fine. Absolutely fine.

A quick glance at my calendar only helped affirm my worth. It was filled, but not for the right reasons. My activities helped me validate my worth and existence and provided a ready answer to the common questions about what I did all day. I made sure I wouldn't have to admit any limits whatsoever. I certainly was keeping score with an invisible and unnamed competitor.

I foolishly thought I was winning.

I was good at it too. Thirty years of hiding negative and positive emotions make one get pretty good at living with a numb heart.

I couldn't believe how comfortable I'd become going through the motions of my life rather than deeply experiencing the full spectrum of emotions in my life. Any time a feeling, positive or negative, tried to rise to the surface, I foolishly pushed it right back where I thought it belonged. Underneath the exterior that I'd created to show everyone that I was fine. I'd even learned how to be the one asking questions to deter anyone from digging too deep inside me.

Fear was growing, however, because I began to sense that I really wasn't fine, and I didn't quite know what to do. The winds that had been behind me for so long seemed to be now shifting and blowing right at my face.

I loved the affirmation I got from all that I did. I'd learned from a very early age that positive affirmation temporarily made everything feel better.

I was also afraid to say no to any requests made of me. Heaven forbid I look like I had limits. But like the frog stuck in a pot of water getting hotter and hotter, I found myself living well beyond my capacity. Even though I suspected it was true, I was terrified to admit it aloud.

For years I was able to cope. Until the number of people that I was seeking to please grew too great. Until I realized I was encouraging my children to be who God created them to be, yet I wasn't doing that for myself. Until I faced the fact that I could articulate what my husband believed about issues even though I didn't know what I believed. Until I didn't even know what I wanted to do on my birthday because I considered everyone else's feelings over mine.

I remember driving home after serving in a ministry at church created to equip people to walk through their ordinary days with Jesus. The ugly truth is that I simply wanted to drive into the garage, shut the door, and head inside the house. You need to realize this wasn't a rare event. It was my new normal. I don't think Jesus would have wanted me to hide from the people in my own backyard.

Yet, the fear of coming up short when I compared myself to many other 'important' women caused me to repeat this hiding and avoidance over and over and over. How had I created a life that wasn't mine? Why was I so afraid to step away from this ministry role?

Deep down I knew the answer. If some of the other women that I had determined were strong and capable could do much more than me, surely, I should be able to do this little bit. I didn't want to appear weak.

What had happened to me? This was so far away from the woman that I thought I was or longed to be.

Losing Linda had been well underway for years, and nobody could help find her but me. Still not wanting to burden anyone with my 'troubles', I kept smiling and skimming through life.

While I had every reason to feel joy, I couldn't. I didn't. Just like trying to shove some clean socks in a drawer already stuffed with dirty ones, I had no room for joy. I was stuffed full of hiding.

The warm summer breezes were beginning to turn to brisk autumn winds. It's not lost on me that those fall winds were blowing over what I deemed most precious to me. My family. The impending changes that I knew were coming were the motivators I embraced to dig a bit deeper into my numb heart so that I could embrace all the parts of life I would have a chance to live.

ROUND AND AROUND

Fall was my favorite season on the farm. I used to stand at the window squinting to see Dad's combine rise over the horizon. Lights shining in the fading daylight declared that all was well.

Months of work and waiting finally paid off for my dad. With a bright red bandana covering my face to protect my lungs from corn dust, I skipped out to meet my dad's wagonful when it arrived in the corn crib. I had a very important job to do.

As Dad unloaded the corn from the wagon onto a vertical conveyor belt, I stood at the top of a fragile wooden ladder to make sure the spout didn't clog and jam as the ears of corn poured into the slatted sides of the corn crib. He was so proud of his fall harvest. I loved bearing witness to the miracle of seeds turning into this abundance of grain.

Few occupations declare the identity and integrity of the seasons like farming. It was obvious to me, even as a little girl, that each season had its own truth. Dad planted corn in late spring. He harvested corn in the fall. His relief was palpable.

Most of the farming year had been covered with anxious optimism. As soon as the calendar flipped to March and the ground began to thaw, my dad prepared to head to the field. Seed to plant had been ordered last winter, and the time to plant seeds was approaching. But just planting these seeds didn't give him any guarantees of a harvest.

Dad and I stood watch on the front porch to watch corn and soybeans grow through the heat and thunderstorms and sunshine of summer. The window to replant any destroyed seeds had come and gone. The weeds that needed to be rooted out had already been destroyed. Unless something went dramatically wrong, we began to count on harvest in the fall. Corn seeds yielded corn. Soybean seeds yielded soybeans. The truth was as simple as that.

It was just time to wait.

But every year it was the same. When the middle of August rolled around, Dad began to pace circles around our kitchen table. For the first time in months, he had nothing more he could do to influence (control) that year's corn and soybeans fields. He'd plowed the soil. He'd planted the seeds. He'd fertilized the tiny plants. He'd cultivated to keep the weeds at bay.

He stood watch as the rain came. He crossed his fingers that the sun would shine. And he celebrated the growth heat and humidity brought. He cared for these babies, these crops, with all his might.

But when there was nothing more he could do, he paced. Had he done enough? Had he done the right things? What would this year's harvest look like?

Even as a little girl, I knew his questions were rhetorical because nothing Mom or I said stopped the questions or the pacing. Common sense would have told Dad to rest a bit before the grueling season of harvest. But, too many questions and too much at stake kept him pacing more laps around the table.

Dad also faced constant comparisons between one farmer and another. Our Sunday drives along the winding country roads grew longer and slower as fall harvest approached. Dad's ability to drive while craning his neck in all directions was his superpower.

"Floyd's beans look a little further along than mine," he admitted quietly. The Pontiac slowed even more. "But I guess my fields look pretty good right?"

The pacing stopped as soon as Dad was able to head to the field on his combine. The waiting was over, and he could finally see the tangible results of another year of farming. Every ounce of his energy was stewarded to the honorable work of filling silos, grain bins, and corn cribs. After doing something that he could control, he could exhale.

It wasn't until I was on the brink of fall in my own life that I thought about Dad's pre-harvest pacing.

My pacing didn't happen around the kitchen table. Instead, I paced by tossing and turning in bed through the wee hours of the night.

What was going to happen when these children of mine no longer lived under our roof? What was I supposed to do with my life? Why didn't I feel joy? Why am I just numb? Why do changes on the horizon create paralyzing fear? Did I miss too many precious moments in the day that just passed?

If my world is going to change, I certainly didn't want to miss out on savoring the present just because I'm worried about the unknown future.

There's the rub. I couldn't pick and choose which emotions my heart could feel. Since I was working so hard to keep from feeling the fear, I was also missing the joy. Layers of plastic were doing their job quite well.

I began to pay attention to the questions that were swirling around in my head as I began my bedtime pacing. My questions were probably very similar to the ones Dad had before he harvested his crops. Had I done enough? Had I done the right things? What will the harvest look like?

I didn't understand how my heart was working yet, but I was smart enough to know that I wasn't feeling the joy that I knew I should feel. Wrapping my fingers to protect them from the cold was a wise decision, but not wrapping my heart! No wonder I didn't feel real anymore. It was time to do some real work to unwrap some more of the layers of plastic I'd accumulated decades earlier.

THAT'S A WRAP

It only took nine words to slice my heart wide open that late October night.

As soon as I walked in the door after my Saturday night date, I knew something horrific had happened. Despair was vividly written on my parents' faces. Tensely, and probably after hours of rehearsing every combination of words, my mom spoke quickly and evenly. The nine words that came out of her mouth shattered my teenage naivety.

"Chris was in a car accident tonight. She's gone."

The next five minutes were blurry.

Mom's tender voice sliced through my fog. "You'd better go to bed and get some sleep. You're going to have a busy next few days."

Eighteen words finished the job.

Those words caused the temperature to drop and the wind chill to rise in my heart. It's one thing to feel cold. But I learned that November night, it's another thing to feel numb.

I don't know how I made it upstairs and into bed. I was completely in shock.

Blinded by my tears, I turned on my night light, grabbed my high school yearbook, and found a picture of Chris. Blonde-haired, blue-eyed, vibrant, joyful Chris. My friend who could make me belly laugh like no other.

She's dead?

I still see my shaking fingers flip through the glossy pages of my yearbook. I longed to talk to someone, but once again having no clue what else to do, I obeyed my mom and tried to get some sleep. Isn't that what a good girl should do?

As I drifted in and out of sleep, I battled my urge to wake up my mom. I desperately needed someone with me, but I was too afraid and raw to risk asking for help. What if she just sent me back to get some sleep?

In a rare moment of doing what I needed versus what I knew was expected, I announced to my parents the next morning that I would not be going to church. My painful determination must have been clearly written on my face because they just quietly nodded their heads. Fortunately, they didn't push back.

The icy seeds of isolation were planting themselves into the cracks of my broken heart.

After my parents left for church, I tried to find some comfort while playing the piano. No luck.

Turning on the radio didn't help either. All the lyrics of the late 70's music seemed to mock me. I couldn't cry. I couldn't sit. I just paced around my kitchen table as my dad modeled. Dead? She's dead?

Intuitively, I knew I had to see the evidence for myself, so I drove to my little town of Newark and knocked at my English teacher's front door. Mrs. Huntley held me while I wept. Shedding the weight of my tears gave me the courage to face the wreckage of the car Chris had been driving. Deep down I had hoped this was all a nightmare. It wasn't. The car was a mangled pile of unrecognized metal. Why had I thought that seeing this was a good idea?

I'd really intended to blurt out my confusion, sadness, and desperation to my parents when I went home. But I'd already gotten so good at being 'fine' over the years, I heard my voice answering detailed questions about her accident and her funeral arrangements instead of digging into my messy heart. My cries buried themselves deeper and deeper and chose to stay silent. The plastic-wrapped and layered very effectively.

My close-knit high school of 200 gathered in the gym the following Monday morning to listen to our well-meaning principal talk about the tragic death of our schoolmate. But I was screaming inside! She was more than that. She was my friend. MY FRIEND! Do you guys understand?

My ears blocked out his monotone speech, and my eyes blocked out the stunned faces seated around me. I honestly didn't care one bit about the dangers of highway driving. I didn't care when her funeral was. Stop telling me the facts. Doesn't anyone care about how I feel? How we all must feel?

As the school meeting droned on, my thoughts raced. Seriously, after this 'school meeting', I must go to my locker and hers is right by mine. She is not there to open hers anymore. Sixteen-year-old girls aren't supposed to die by the side of the road. Who will I sit by in trigonometry? What about her dreams? How does her family do this? Why didn't God stop the accident? So many thoughts. So deep inside me. I didn't think I should voice all those swirling words. Instead, I went to my locker, got my trigonometry book, and obediently sat through class.

It's a mystery how a heart can scream at the same time it's silent.

Funeral day. I sat near the front of her little country church flanked by my girlfriends. Staring at her lifeless body, I knew I should cry. But no matter how hard I tried to muster up some tears, I was empty.

I felt so guilty. Why couldn't I cry? What was wrong with me? Even worse was the dark truth that I wanted to cry so my parents would see my grief from their vantage point in the balcony. Maybe that would create a space for me to talk about how sad I was. While I knew they cared deeply, I also knew that we wouldn't speak of this tragic death after the funeral.

So, I just pushed through one day after another. Whenever my confusion or anger or sadness began to poke around too loudly, I just found another piece of plastic to wrap around my heart. That was oh so much easier than admitting I wasn't ok. At least for a little while.

But not really.

My dad paid close attention to the impact of frost on his corn and soybeans each fall. Freezing temperatures before the grain reaches maturity can create havoc upon the crops. Yield is reduced, and full ripening is prevented. Farmers hate early frost.

But frost at the right time serves its purpose in the fall. It kills off the stems and leaves displaying the true harvest grain.

The numbness I was feeling after Chris's accident was begging me to admit the grief and sadness and confusion hidden inside of it. Even as I tried to stomp it out, the invitation of truthful vulnerability was present. However, I didn't know what to do with the numbness, and like an early frost, it prevented a full ripening of the grief in that season.

PLAYING IT SAFE

My mom frequently told me that I could do anything I wanted to.

She was right - at least for most of my childhood through most of my high school. If I wanted to do something, I was able to do it.

Until my piano teacher moved away just months before I was to audition for a spot in the Wheaton College Conservatory. I knew that without a teacher and severely lagging in music theory, I had little chance of being accepted. So, sitting on my bed, which was covered with daunting audition requirements, I had a choice to make.

The brave thing at that moment would have been to walk into the kitchen and tell my mom I was scared. That I might fail. Perhaps we could have even devised a plan B. But, no.

I lied.

I told Mom that I'd changed my mind and didn't want to pursue music at the conservatory. Instead, I wanted to apply for general admission to Wheaton College. So that's what I did.

Failure averted! Check. Phew!!!

In retrospect, not attending the conservatory was a better choice for me, but I still hate the reason why I didn't pursue music. That moment of avoiding any risk of failing established a pattern that haunted me for decades. Coupled with my inability to feel negative emotions like sadness or grief, I had turned onto a rough road without even knowing it.

Now, I want to be clear that my mom's words to me were 100% intended to be encouragement. And in many ways, they were. But I had not learned how to fail. Or that it was ok to fail. Or that it was brave to try things outside of my comfort zone.

During the time of my life when patterns become deeply rooted, I learned to play it safe. I got more comfortable lying about my dreams rather than take any risks. I was well on my way to avoid any vulnerability about fearing failure that I would possibly feel. Just another layer of plastic to neatly bundle up my heart.

But what is reaped when misunderstood messages are mistakenly sowed in the tender fertile ground of a young heart? When 'don't feel' and 'don't fail' begin to take root? When they are mulled over and over and over without correction from someone wiser than me?

I entered adulthood believing those simple and innocent words far too long. While they had been intended for good, I twisted them to a million broken pieces in my mind.

How do I go about admitting to someone - anyone - that I am so afraid to fail? To disappoint anyone?

I couldn't ignore that nagging question on the last day of our homeschool year one late May. As I stood in front of my homeschool cabinet, I barely had the energy to shove all the books and papers inside so that I could close the door on what I considered a failed school year. While spring was at its peak with beauty and exuberant growth, I was exhausted in the worst possible way.

I officially, yet internally, declared myself an utter failure. As a wife. As a mom. As a homeschool teacher. As a ministry volunteer. As a friend. As a daughter. Yadda, yadda, yadda. Years of pressure I'd placed on myself bubbled up into a white flag that I was waving to nobody in particular.

I'd failed. There. I said it.

Nothing happened. No explosions. No withdrawal of love. Nothing.

I couldn't keep pasting the smile on my face. I was too weary from not having my inside world match my outside world.

That moment of truth at the school cabinet drove me to a counselor's office. When I sat there, I didn't quite know where to begin, but I did say, "I have a great life, but I'm so frustrated, impatient, and miserable on the inside."

Then I told my counselor the following story where I knew I utterly had failed.

Debralyn, my daughter, was about 10 years old and had repeatedly asked me to sew her a native American dress for over a year. I'd already made a buckskin costume for her older brother, and obviously, she wanted to join in the fun. So many nights I crawled into bed with her sweet little voice echoing in my heart.

Even though sewing this costume would take about two hours, I didn't have the energy to find two hours to spare. When my counselor saw the failure shooting out of my eyes, she looked me squarely and told me the truth.

"Linda, there are dozens of people who will line up to assume your ministry role at church. Debralyn only has one mom who can make that dress. Your choice."

She saw the real me that I couldn't even see yet. She knew which choice would reflect who I had been created to be.

I was face to face with my limits and for the first time, and I felt permission to have them.

Even though I was terrified to resign from my volunteer role at church, I admitted that I wasn't living my true life with Jesus. I was living a life to perform perfectly for Jesus. But wasn't living with Him. No longer would I assume I needed to continue simply because she successfully handled her responsibilities while raising three children. But she wasn't me, and I wasn't her.

I liked what I reflected in the mirror when I held that little suede brown dress I'd sewn for Debralyn. Joy. Richness. Authenticity.

I wish that simply sewing this little outfit fixed the brokenness in my heart. While it was a very good start toward healing, I still knew that my inside and outside didn't match up. In my haunted moments of silence, I knew that what I was displaying was too far away from the state of my insides. I still thought I needed to be fine. Capable. Perfect. And I was so tired of feeling like I had to do something to prove something to someone. I was tired of feeling like I either had to perform or to hide.

Here I thought I was living my life. But the truth was I had lost it. My life experience was trying to talk to me. Thankfully, I recognized that the changes flooding over me were actually echoing that message.

WHOEVER 'SHE' IS

Truth time. Somewhere along the way, I learned how to compare myself to others, and I got really good at it. For simplicity's sake, her name is 'she.'

My first 'she' had long, wavy blonde hair and saucer-like brown eyes. She had adorable pigtails that cascaded into the most beautiful banana curls. Her Barbie collection included the Barbie motor home.

I didn't have any of those things. My hair was straight and dirty blonde and my hazel eyes hid behind tortoiseshell glasses. Pigtails were out of the question, and my banana curls looked rotten. My Barbies only traveled in a motor home when they went to her house.

I did what any six-year-old girl would do. I pulled her pigtails during an argument while riding home from school on the bus. I pretended to not care at all about her Barbies and sabotaged our playtimes. So there. I win.

Over the years, my 'she' morphed often. But there were some common elements to all of them. Each of them was skinnier, more fashionable, and had prettier hair. They could do cartwheels which put them on the cheerleading squad. They appeared to know how to fit in when I felt a little more than awkward. It didn't matter to me that I could play the piano or ace any test that came my way. I just wanted my outside to look like them.

But here's the irony. I didn't want to look just like them. I simply wanted to feel stylish and confident and cute. Because in the nooks and crannies of my mind, I'd foolishly concluded that's how they felt.

I determined that I'd find my own way to distinguish myself, so I learned how to sew. We didn't have many places to shop where I grew up. And going to a shopping mall was as unlikely as finding a deal on Amazon or inspiration on Pinterest in those days. Remember I didn't want to look like everyone else. Just someone else.

When *Seventeen* magazine's Back to School issue came out in August, I spent hours pouring over the clothing, hair, and make-up styles. If I could just mimic one of the looks highlighted on those glossy pages, I was fairly certain I'd feel better. To be honest, I'd become a bit embarrassed that I was sewing my own clothes as that had begun to represent my perception that I couldn't fit easily into cute little junior-sized clothes found in the few stores we had.

Something needed to be done if I wanted to 'fit' in and compete with 'her.'

When I was sixteen, I saved my babysitting money and decided to splurge, not on fabric to sew, but on a Bobbie Brooks plaid skirt and vest set sold at a nearby boutique. It was a rare treat to shop there and even rarer to walk out of that store with a bag of new clothes slung over my arm. I felt invincible, and I am not exaggerating! I FINALLY was replicating what *Seventeen* magazine portrayed. I certainly hoped I would feel what I thought this outfit promised me.

I tried on my darling prize day after day after day rehearsing for my first day of school. I was so confident and proud and eager to show up to school wearing my 'store-bought' outfit.

Until I arrived in my advanced biology class and sat right behind the boutique owner's daughter. You know where this is going, don't you?

She was wearing the same Bobbie Brooks plaid skirt and vest set. But it looked so much better on her slimmer body. Her long blonde hair casually swept over her shoulders make her vest pop far better than mine. Her make-up was impeccable and highlighted all the right colors of the plaid.

'She' won again. I was devastated and never wore that outfit again.

My external appearance clearly mattered more than it should, but I didn't understand all of that then. All I knew was that I needed to work harder on how I looked on the outside. So, I skipped meals, drank diet 7-Up, and tried to buy the 'right' clothes instead of simply sewing all of them. This was more of my college prep program than advanced chemistry or advanced placement tests.

While my 'smarts' qualified to me attend Wheaton College, I was in no way prepared for my first taste of something called 'suburban affluence.' It didn't take me long to realize that the clothing I had sewn or purchased with my hard-earned money didn't measure up to how I wanted to present myself once I arrived at college. With a full closet, but a sad heart, I tried to compensate. But I didn't do too well.

'She' was everywhere.

'She' was across the hall from my dorm room wearing fur coats and high heeled boots.

'She' was my roommate who was athletic and looked fantastic in Adidas gear or Levi jeans.

'She' was my friend who could throw on a floral cotton dress, long ivory sweater, heels, and make guys' heads turn.

'She' was a part of the Florida girl group.

'She' was a cheerleader.

'She' dated the football players.

I'd clearly drunk a long sip of the 'Kool-Aid' which could turn deadly for me.

I began to be ashamed of my homemade clothes even though I loved to sew and was darn good at it. I grew increasingly uncomfortable with my body and eating late-night pizzas with my college suitemates didn't help. If only I could get some of the time back that I wasted trying to be just like every 'she' that I had decided was better than me.

After I married Ron and we had more resources, I traded my sewing machine for the mall. Receiving affirmation for a well-accessorized outfit fed the monster that had made itself quite at home inside me. But I overspent and overbought. Just when I thought I was pretty comfortable with a certain style, I'd see another 'she' wearing another style and decided I needed to try that too. Instead of being me, I was projecting myself like 'she' did. I copied every 'she' and her style I deemed important.

It didn't just stop with my own body and its coverings. It invaded my home as well.

I'm naturally hospitable and love having people in my suburban home, but I soon learned that I was intimidated entertaining people that I perceived had more or did the hospitality thing better than me. My mom used to demonstrate that there was always room for another person at the table and that there was always enough food to feed more. But her voice began to be drowned out by other voices telling me that everything needed to be perfect. The focus I had placed on my external appearance had spread into the very home that I loved to live in and share with others. I hated this feeling but wasn't confident enough to kill it yet.

You'll never guess what my biggest clue that I had crossed over into the 'other side' was.

It was my feet.

I rarely wore shoes when I ran around the yard as a little girl on the farm. I loved the feel of the grass tickling my toes. Even the occasional bee stings, sharp thistles, or nasty slivers didn't stop me from running free in the grass or up and down our gravel lane.

But 'she' would never do that in suburbia. So, I put on shoes to walk around the yard or even walk out to get the mail. I felt so fake and artificial, but I cared more about what 'she' thought than what was true about me. My feet were pristine, but I clearly wasn't

38

true to me. I was covering some important parts of me up, and I was getting tired of it. Something needed to change.

TRUE COLORS

The beauty of running on the same wooded path all year long is that many of the trees become familiar to me, especially when they show off their colors in the fall. The nature lover inside of me just had to know why some fall leaves turn golden, others red, and still others a dark russet brown.

It's actually quite simple, but also mysteriously magical. As summer meanders into fall, at least in my part of the world, the amount of daylight diminishes as the temperatures drop. These two changes signal the trees to prepare for winter. The trees go on a diet or literally stop eating which stops the flow of chlorophyll to the leaves.

Here's where it gets interesting!

Xanthophyll has been hiding under the green in the leaves of the trees that turn yellow, gold, or orange in the fall. This yellow pigment appears only after the green fades away. Did you catch this? The yellow has been there all along. It's only because of the changes occurring in the fall that we finally see something other than green.

The leaves that show off the deep red and magenta colors are a bit fickler. Their colors are most brilliant only when fall temperatures range between freezing and 45 degrees AND there is plenty of sunshine. These colors don't disappear in quite the same way as our yellow friends hide.

Instead, some of the glucose produced when the tree manufactured its food stays trapped in the leaves. Then the chlorophyll disappears, and the glucose reddens because of anthocyanin, a red pigment catalyst that was always there. I love that it's the same pigment that makes roses and geraniums red. Did Alice in Wonderland know that?

Finally, there are those oaks. For all the majesty and strength of an oak tree, they are rather unremarkable in the fall. Their leaves turn brown instead of glorious. But the fading oak leaves are critical for the tree to remain strong. They are literally cleaning the tree of all its waste now that the chlorophyll is gone. Once their chores are done, they turn brown and fall to the forest floor. It's all rather ordinary, but extremely critical for the health of the tree.

All this science about the emerging fall colors spoke deeply to me as I looked, not only at the trees, but also at me.

Why have I let whoever my 'she' is define who I think I should be? Why have I allowed whoever my 'she' is define how I think I need to look? Why in an attempt to be affirmed or accepted have I denied my true self to show? Why have I perhaps not even remembered who I am?

As my life became less predictable and controllable, I realized that I wanted the truth about me to shine through just like the trees demonstrated. Instead of going through the motions and putting layer upon layer of someone else's life upon mine, I wanted to discover and display what was underneath my 'chlorophyll.' If I didn't get serious about discovering me without the influence of 'she', I probably wouldn't even recognize what would be eventually exposed inside of me.

At this point, I resonated the most with the oak because I knew I had a lot of cleaning to do on the inside. It certainly wasn't going to happen overnight, but over the long haul, perhaps change would occur! I still entered rooms and quickly assessed how I measured up compared to the other 'she' that I saw. Deeply embedded patterns are hard to break, but I took some hope from those little acorns that slowly and steadily turn into majestic oaks.

And one of my first steps was to take off my shoes and walk barefoot across my yard. In broad daylight. In front of people. If you'd been there, you'd have seen a big smile on my face.

BINDWEED, CHOKEBERRIES, LIES

I didn't know they were invading, digging, and spreading their roots more deeply into my garden summer after summer. If my garden looked lush and thick above ground, I didn't really pay attention to a few irritating vines and straggling branches poking their noses into the mix. I just plucked the tops off the vines and pruned back the tiny sticks of the chokeberries. I was far too ignorant to realize that I needed to get on my hands and knees and dig out all the roots. Tucked amongst the abundance of perennials and lilacs and shrubs, I figured that if I plucked the tops off those uninvited guests from time to time, the winter cold would take care of the rest.

It is the natural cycle of things that each fall, my garden blooms would fade, and my backyard flowering bushes would lose their leaves. It isn't lost on me that the bindweed and chokeberries lingered a long time after the beauty of the perennials. It was as if they were giving me a chance to clean them out, but honestly, who wants to 'harvest' weeds in the fall? I certainly didn't. So, I ignored them for yet another season. Can you catch where I'm heading?

The fact that bindweed is commonly known as morning glory is such a lie. There is nothing glorious about it. This weed multiplies, then spreads, and finally takes over. It always looks like it is winning.

Bindweed makes itself at home by sinking roots as much as nine feet deep into the soil and can stay on as an unwanted guest for up to 20 years. Bindweed grows along the ground until it contacts other plants or structures and spreads over anything in its path. The stems covered with arrow-shaped leaves wrap around any object as it grows. In my garden, those objects were other plants. Can you guess what the objects were in my life?

I would have thought the freezing temperatures and inches of snow would have killed off the bindweed and chokeberries. I didn't want to 'waste' my gardening energy trying to root out weeds. Yet, each spring, these bindweed vines arrived more vigorous and prolific, and the chokeberries were beginning to compete in height with my other little shrubs and trees. My strategy wasn't working.

When my strong and vibrant rose of Sharon shrub began to die, I paid attention. "I really need to get to that," I told myself over and over all summer long.

But, for me, it's much more fun to pick flowers and pull the occasional dandelion than do the heavy, hard work of digging out invasive weeds. I was too hurried to follow the maze of bindweed through to where it originated in the dirt. Instead, I just grabbed what I could and then turned my attention to the more enjoyable parts of gardening. And trust me. I certainly wasn't going to get the shovel out to try to dig out chokeberries.

Those little winding vines and spotted chokeberry branches taunted me. If my garden was to live or even thrive, I had to devote some time in the fall to do the hard work of digging out those ugly killers. Taking advantage of the changing landscape, I was able to more clearly see the bindweed and chokeberries because apparently in Illinois, weeds live longer than perennials.

So, I got down on my knees and instead of simply yanking out the top of a bindweed vine, I followed its stem all the way to its insertion into the ground. You must realize it was still wrapped around the stems of whatever flower that had been in its path, so I unwound and unwound. Gently, of course. But, with some perseverance. Because I wanted to find where its entrance into the soil was so that I could dig it out. That was the only way to rid my

46

garden of all the bindweed. It took a long time, and it honestly wasn't that satisfying. I love to see concrete results, but in this case, all I saw was the plant that blocked what should have been there all along. It wasn't until the next growing season that I could breathe a sigh of relief. The strangling hold of the bindweed was gone. Hurrah?

Then I moved to the chokeberries. They were a bit trickier to discover in the fall because they had been camouflaged amongst the shrubs all summer long. But, their desire to be showy was their downfall. Their leaves were the last to drop, and they typically grew taller than the shrub they had attacked. Because of that, I was able to identify their spotted limbs and follow their limbs all the way down to their roots.

Showing off was their downfall.

I'll admit that I used a variety of methods to kill those darn chokeberries, and I still battle them every year, but now they are no longer disguised from me. I can recognize a chokeberry growing amongst the lilacs and viburnums and red twigged dogwood. And now I know how to get rid of them. Ah-ha!

My fall gardening isn't nearly as fun as my spring or summertime gardening. In this season of transition, I must do all that I can to be ready for the next season of growth. And because of the proximity of my garden to the woods, I have to dig out bindweed and chokeberries. And lies.

This isn't unlike what I began to realize I was going to have to do with the lies that had woven their way into the soil of my heart. If debris accumulates, when will we clean it out? What will I do to strengthen my 'healthy' roots before the winter season arrives? If the bindweed and chokeberries represent anything to me, they represent the reality that I must clean out the lies so that I can live in the healthy center of what is true.

I had to be a hero for myself and dig out and sift out the lies that were strangling my ability to live my life. Just like the bindweed and chokeberries were trying to thwart my gardening efforts, my lies were trying to thwart my living efforts.

What were the roots entangling in my soul? Feeling, failing, and being less than 'she' was trying to destroy me. Just as persistence and dedication were needed to rid my garden of bindweed and chokeberries, honesty and vulnerability were needed to detangle my life from the lies that I had let take root. Upon reflection, the honesty of fall and the transitions in my life served me extremely well!

THAWING?

The term hoar frost is believed to have originated from a German word meaning graying and old. It was thought to describe the color of an old man's beard. I'd never heard of the term 'hoar frost' until I experienced the following.

It all began one morning when I'd had enough. Fine was calling my name, but I knew it was all a lie.

Autumn winds were changing in what I deemed most precious to me. My family. While it's a long story that unfolded over several years, it's actually quite simple.

My strong, fiercely capable and dependable husband began to signal that he had limits. Trust me, I was not comfortable with this. His word pictures suggested that he felt like he was trying to land a 747 jet at a tiny airport. He had no way out of the plane until he tried to land on an inadequate runway. Was he about to crash?

I was knee-deep in homeschooling our three children and wasn't too eager to push pause on anything that was already written on my agenda in pen.

But Ron needed some emotional support. Emotional, you say? Even in my middle age, I knew about as much about handling his 'negative' emotions as I did about landing a 747 jet. I was a little more than terrified on the inside, but I'd gotten comfortable at looking fine on the outside.

I didn't know how to walk through the pain of a thawing heart. It really hurt. I ached as I watched while Ron worked so hard to get better. It was a kind of two steps forward and one step back kind of journey. I don't like one step back. My motherly instinct was on high alert as I wanted to handle our family struggles with authenticity while protecting our children's innocent hearts. Honestly, I just wanted everything to be ok again. Or like it used to be. I was weary. I was tired. I was mad. Every time I thought we were on the brink of 'fine' again, there'd be another setback. I didn't understand it. Here we were trying to lean into doing life God's way and making good choices, yet He had not allowed 'fine' to return when and where I thought He should.

With these thoughts simmering in my mind, I headed out to run through the forest preserve. The hoar frost was everywhere. The tall grasses and majestic trees lining my forest trail were clothed in glistening diamonds. Because it was a frosty late fall morning, ice crystals clung for dear life to every branch and blade of grass. The early morning sunlight reflecting off these clear jewels blinded me. Normally the beauty would have taken my breath away, but this morning I was merely irritated that it was so bright as I ran toward the rising sun. The outside brightness contradicted my internal darkness. Even the metal railing along the bridge was covered in frozen drops. Pounding my feet on the concrete seemed to lessen the angry voices screaming inside my head.

The hoar frost began to overcome my focus.

I slowly became aware of dripping sounds while the warmth of the sun gradually melted crystal after crystal of ice. Drops were falling all around me and begging me to pay attention to them. Could it be God felt my sadness? Quite possibly.

Now I was outside in the woods with the tears of God raining down on me. He knew I was in pain. He knew that I was longing to thaw. He knew that I didn't even have a clue what was in store for me. But he had frosted the trees, grasses, and even the high wires in advance to let me know that He would be with me through the melting process. He would hold my fragile, frightened heart in His tender hands. He would cry for me as I faced the current and future winds blowing change throughout my life.

Even though this is now years ago, I see it vividly. He showed up to write a new story smack dab in the middle of my life. I was awed. Humbled. Scared.

Anyone looking into our family from the outside would have declared that we were fine. But it was becoming harder to fall or stay asleep almost every night. I had this nagging feeling that things were changing, and I had no idea how to embrace any of it.

I began to take some risks for the first time in my life by admitting that my life wasn't fine. I was met mostly with intellectual responses or awkwardness or painful push back. Perhaps I wasn't well-practiced at communicating the less desirable emotions such as fear and anger. Perhaps I wasn't particularly wise in who to open up with. Yes, it was hard. But I was determined that I was going to land this huge plane of truth.

As Ron changed and reordered his life in healthier ways, I cheered him on. Yes, I kept bumping into him. The familiar was embedded in me. I guess I was going to have to do something about this heart of mine. Numb wasn't working for me anymore.

I had to begin scanning my life. My heart broke over and over each time I saw someone I loved struggle with limits. But maybe it's better to feel something, even if it is hard? I wasn't quite sure.

I hated it when my vulnerability was met with blank stares or dismissals. Maybe I should have just kept my mouth shut, I reasoned. Why throw off the balance of the way I'd established my relationships? You know. Where I was the one that was fine? Something didn't feel right about that either.

A wise woman told me that I was going to need to learn how to dance a new dance with my husband. His dance steps were changing. He was growing through his stuck points. I had a choice to make. I could either plant myself at the edge of the dance floor with a 'fine' grin on my face and muscles tensing throughout my body or I could begin a journey of uncovering my heart. As scary as it sounded, I knew what the best answer would be.

It was time for me to embrace the lessons of fall.

I needed to discover who I truly was.

To understand what I needed to hold on to and let go of. I needed to see what seeds I'd sown that shouldn't be growing in my heart and rip them out.

I needed to learn how to be grateful for my real life.

I carried some 'loaded' words with me as I stood on the brink of reordering my life and my heart.

Motivated by the story of the velveteen rabbit, I admitted to a ministry friend that somehow, I had lost my life along the way of living it. I was tired of hiding me from myself and from others.

I was so scared to hear her response. I didn't have it in me to have one more person try to fix me or shame me or embarrass me after I took the risk of being vulnerable.

I love that I can begin this next sentence with 'but'.

'But' just like the little boy in *The Velveteen Rabbit*, she encouraged the real parts of me to shine through the false image I'd worked so hard to create.

She grabbed my hands and looked deeply into my downcast eyes. With deep emotion, she said, "I can't wait to meet Linda when you find her again."

My heart echoed her sentiment. I can't wait to meet her either.

CLEAN FLOORS AND POTATO CHIPS

I eagerly wrote out how many minutes I needed to run each day for eighteen weeks on a sheet of paper and taped it to the inside of my kitchen cabinet. If I could just cross off each daily run - cross off - cross off - day after day, I would be able to run a marathon. Wow! Sounds simple.

I was careful about who I talked about my decision to run a marathon. It's hard to believe that I was the girl who hid in the trunk of a car during high gym classes because I HATED running! I HATED it because I told myself I wasn't good at it.

But over the years, I couldn't get running a marathon out of my mind.

I knew had to start small. I ran up and down my little suburban street while my babies napped. On Saturdays, I explored more adventurous routes, but I still felt rather feeble in my running attempts.

But, over time I was able to run marathons! All because of my kitchen floor and a handful of potato chips.

Huh?

My kitchen floor, first of all, mirrored an external picture of my heart. I could spend half an hour on my hands and knees washing my floor only to spill on it just moments later.

What I hadn't realized until a few years ago was that I was sabotaging my own heart by washing my kitchen floor instead of paying attention to my real feelings. In fact, you could say that the main reason I had a clean kitchen floor was because I was trying to outrun my feelings.

It was when Ron and I got one of 'those' dreaded phone calls from a leader of our high school youth group. Our daughter, Debralyn, was away at winter camp.

"Debralyn fell on the ice. She's broken a tooth. We think you need to get her."

A broken tooth was a gross understatement. When we saw her, we drove her straight to the closest emergency room.

But on the way to that hospital, Ron got a call from his mom asking if he could help transport his dad to their local emergency room. What does a dad/son do at that moment? I felt so sorry for the struggle he was experiencing.

After a very tiring and emotional night, I woke up early the next morning. Ron was already on his way to the hospital to be with his parents, and Debralyn was still asleep. I had a few minutes before I had to wake her up to head to a 7 am dentist appointment to address her teeth issues. The dentist had already visited her in the wee Saturday night hours in the ER but needed to work with her again that morning.

So, I did what any logical thinking woman would do.

I began to wash my kitchen floor. It wasn't even dirty.

Over the course of the next 14 days, I had 18 different trips to doctors, dentists, oral surgeons, and hospitals. My lifelong girlfriend also died.

I washed my kitchen floor so many times during those two weeks. I lost count at fourteen.

I wish I could say that I used my scrubbing time to pray, but that would be a lie. I was actually more concerned about trying to create some order and control in the middle of what I perceived as chaos. I was longing for the day when it would be all over and everything would be back to normal.

As my kitchen floor began to groan under yet another cleaning, I began to realize that I was hiding my fear and sadness under my mop and spray cleaner. It was easier to just clean that little bit of my kingdom on earth rather than sit with all that was so uncomfortable and sad and scary in my heart.

That season of doctors and hospitals seems long ago, and I'm still waiting for the 'chaos' to stop.

Just like the kitchen floor that keeps getting dirty. My world will keep getting dirty until there is no life happening on top of it.

This Facebook status slapped my face.

"Making order out of chaos... a lifelong endeavor."

On the surface, my friend was talking about putting pencils and athletic socks where they belonged. She'd cleaned out a closet and filled a garbage bag. Once that was full, there'd be other things to clean and eliminate.

I've been thinking a lot about the deeper meaning that I'm certain she intended to imply. I realized that too much of me keeps waiting for the chaos to go away...for my heart to not have to deal with junk falling on it, much like hoping crumbs stop falling on my kitchen floor.

The external is easy for me. It's easy to clean my kitchen floor.

It's paying attention to the inside stuff that is much more challenging to clean out.

Then I remembered what one of my running buddies told me when I told her my shoulders were super sore from running. Not my legs, mind you, my shoulders. From running. You know, from running on my legs.

"When you're running, pretend you're holding a potato chip in each hand. Don't you dare crush them."

It took me a while to believe her, but the proof was in the 'potato chip' so to speak.

If you're not a runner, you may not understand, so let me explain. And if you are a runner, it's totally worth a try.

55

Running requires much more than putting one foot in front of the other, even though that is VERY important. Running also requires much more than crazy lung capacity and the ability to drink from a tiny cup while moving relatively quickly.

Running with even a small level of pleasure requires the ability to keep your body relaxed while at the same time expending enormous amounts of energy. Someone must have discovered that the tensing begins at the core and then moves out along the shoulders, down the arms, and into the fingers. Who knew that squeezing fingers together makes any difference on a run?

The next time I went out for my long run, I realized that my fists were in fact clenched. My arms were mechanically swinging back and forth, and my shoulders were hunched up like an accordion before release. Far too much energy was being unnecessarily spent in my upper body.

By relaxing my fingers and trying not to crack my pretend, fragile potato chip, the fluidity began to move up my arms and spread into my shoulders and neck. I surprisingly had more energy left for my legs to do what they were being asked to do.

Eventually holding my hands loosely became my habit. When I began to feel fatigued, my first check was my fingers. Not my hydration or my pace or even the wind. Just my hands.

Do.Not.Fracture.The.Potato.Chip.

Later that year I completed my first Chicago marathon. When I saw the photo of me crossing the finish line, I immediately noticed that my hands were open instead of clenched. I'll never know if that helped me finish the race, but I do know that I haven't run with my fists clenched since then.

Fall is all about letting go. Of holding loosely. Of anticipation. Of expecting something to come from our efforts.

But I was also challenged to release my grip on the outcome. We come into this world holding on tightly with our babyish instinct. Then we spend the rest of our life learning how to let go of our control. That is the beauty of running with a potato chip in each hand that I refuse to crush.

I've often wished it was as easy to let go of my need to control as it is to not crush a potato chip. My family's story was continuing to unfold, and it was driving me crazy that I didn't know what the next chapter would hold. Ironically, I wouldn't let anyone spoil the ending of a movie before I watched it, and I never read the last chapter of a book first.

But in my real life, I wanted to know what these changes were going to mean to the people I love and to me. What would the various finish lines look like? Or would I just have to keep running with open hands?

I pass by the maple trees in my neighborhood most days without giving them a second look. It wasn't until the rays of the morning sun lit it up one chilly fall morning that I couldn't resist opening my hands and raising them to the sky. Golden leaves painted against the brilliant blue autumn sky took my breath away. I hadn't noticed the subtle changes the leaves were undergoing until they'd reached the pinnacle of their vibrancy.

Is that part of my answer? Instead of looking for a finish line, I should look for the beauty occurring in and shining through change? Instead of thinking I could possibly control any of the outcomes, I should just open my hands and embrace what comes?

Perhaps it's time to replace all my old messages with the simple truth that I need to let it go.

PART II

The Rabbit sighed. He thought it would be a long time before this magic called Real happened to him. He longed to become Real, to know what it felt like; and yet the idea of growing shabby and losing his eyes and whiskers was rather sad. He wished that he could become it without these uncomfortable things happening to him.

The Velveteen Rabbit

I SURRENDER

It's not until fall that we can see the brownish corn stalks holding ripened ears of corn.

It's not until fall that we can see the branches and nests that have been hiding beneath the abundant green leaves.

It's not until fall that we really see the stems that once supported the gorgeous flower heads.

It's the 'letting go' or the 'holding loosely' season of fall.

Subtle, yet daily changes in light and temperature give those little brave stalks, branches, or stems the courage they need to give up control and surrender to the next season's changes.

Why does it seem so effortless for the leaves and stalks to let go in the fields, the forest preserve, or even in my own backyard? Why does all this seamless letting go of control create such a struggle internally for me?

All the false beliefs and misinterpreted messages I'd accumulated for decades screamed at me to make sure everyone was ok. That I didn't fail or lose. That I secure a safe place in my world. Without those structures, I wasn't quite sure who I was. And at the same time, I was beginning to see changes on the horizon. How in the world could I embrace my own personal autumn authentically?

Answers to that question came in surprising places.

My oldest son, Jordan, was registered to take a college-prep exam at our local high school. As his homeschool teacher/mom, I naturally assumed I should accompany him and his friend into the unfamiliar halls of the high school. After parking the car, the three of us entered the hallway maze and wound our way to the testing destination.

A basket of yellow #4 pencils was my clue that we were now in the right place. As soon as Jordan found the SAT room 'gatekeeper,' he casually told me I was free to go. What he really meant to say was that he wanted me to go. He wanted to do this all without his mom.

"I'm good. I don't need you," he nonchalantly declared.

His words were kind yet determined. Somewhere between his mouth and my heart, I felt the fall winds blowing. Something new was emerging from the shadows of summertime abundance.

Fortunately, I made it back to my car before my tears flowed like an open water faucet. What? He doesn't need me?

I wasn't ready for all our investment into his confidence and character to come out in just one sentence. Even if he didn't need me, I wanted him to need me. Can I get an amen?

How do I transition from being the mom my kids 'need' to become the mom that supports, challenges, and encourages them? I was stunned that this idea had never occurred to me before. I guess I'd entered a new and unfamiliar in-between time of mothering, and it was very uncomfortable.

Nature has those 'in-between' times. I began to wonder if I had what it took to live authentically in the 'in-between' time between holding on and letting go.

I'd watched the early morning light wave its magic wand over changing seasons most of my life. Summertime breezes blowing through the proud prairie grasses gave way to chilly winds touching gorgeous layers of orange, gold, red or brown. It's so magical to witness the 'in-between' outdoors yet so frightening to experience inside my home.

The endless green of summer had transformed into abundant fall textures. Each clump of colors told its unique story. Those textures invited me to see what was happening in the nooks and crannies of fall.

Patches of Queen Anne's lace still dotted the prairie landscape. They stood with their blooms casually folded up toward the sky, brown and strong. What beautiful stems now hold these little fragile balls of brown. The summer's lacy white flowers atop the stems had made me overlook the beauty of their important support structures.

The coneflowers had dropped their faded pink petals, yet they still stood erect and proud like guards across the fields. How strong those stems must have been as they withstood the summer winds and storms. They still held their seed heads and will continue to offer them as a food source for the woodland birds until next spring.

And don't get me started on the maple trees. Or cottonwoods. Or walnut trees. Those trees which had been a haven for birds' nests, squirrel nests, and woodpecker holes. All under the cover of leaves. But as their leafy green leaves began to lose ground to the hidden colors, they also began to shrivel around their edges. Space was created to begin to see the amazing and intricate designs of the branches that had supported and nurtured those leaves all summer. The gnarly, intertwined, strong branches had unceremoniously performed their duties but stayed hidden in secret behind the fluttering leaves.

Newly created beautiful gaps provided stunning views of the support they had provided. Those stems and branches literally held everything together, but it wasn't until fall that they received the recognition they deserve.

Is any of this any different than Jordan declaring he didn't really need me to help him take his next step at the local high school? Are some of those unique textures just beginning to emerge in his life? In our relationship? Maybe family life isn't just lush and all shades of summer green anymore. But maybe we can see some distinguishing supports during the changes.

I began to repeat over and over to myself that it was ok to begin embracing changes arriving in my family. Even if I experienced bouts of sadness or loss or fear, it was still ok.

In my own journey to embracing the real me, I intentionally invited fall to teach me how to handle changes in my life and in our family's story. I needed to acknowledge the diligent growth, albeit hidden, of all the supports my husband and I had put in place to help our family thrive. While it still was more natural for me to think in terms of 'we,' I needed to let them separate in healthy ways into the 'you' and 'me.' So that 'we' could be healthy and authentic.

Isn't that what part of my role as a mom was all along? I needed to move behind the scenes yet stand sturdy and strong enough for my children to attach to my branch while they grew. And then to detach. The detaching still seems like a surprise and a little bit like bait and switch. But so critical. In my own season of fall, I needed to mirror the trees and learn how to let go of my children. The health for each of us depends upon it.

YOU TOO?

After an hour, I've only seen one person drive by my house, which is unusual even on my quiet street. Apparently, I'm the only one around who decided to venture out and let the heat penetrate my skin. Granted I'm sitting. In the shade. With a water bottle.

But I'm out here letting myself feel even if I get uncomfortable.

I wish it was as easy to do that in all parts of life. I usually do all I can do to avoid anything uncomfortable.

If I'm hot, I turn on the air conditioning. If I'm thirsty, I sip water. If I'm hungry, I grab some food. If I'm bored, I pick up a book. If I'm cold, I grab my sweatshirt. Those are the easy ones.

But what do I do if I'm lonely? What do I do if I'm afraid? What do I do when I feel sad? I wish I could say that every time I immediately called a trusted friend or found the perfect scripture reference to recalibrate my soul.

Instead, I am much more comfortable avoiding those uncomfortable emotions by checking Facebook. By buying something new. By 'running' an errand. By literally running. By washing my kitchen floor.

When sculptors create their magnificent works of art, they need to cut away anything that would get in the way of the image they were trying to create. That seemed like a worthy concept to model. What do I need to cut away to create the me that I want to create?

An important chunk to remove first and foremost was living out the lie that I was always fine.

Two of my girlfriends spent a day exploring some of the places of my childhood. We drove to one of my hometown spots, and as we sat over soup and sandwiches, I took a risk. I asked them for some honest reflection of what they saw in my life. But that was the easy part.

I got honest by letting them behind the curtain into the struggles of my life. They heard parts of my life that were hard. Where I hated what I saw reflected when I looked in the mirror. That I was intentionally naming my lies and seeking to be authentic, but how uncomfortable all of that was.

Then I told them I didn't know who I was now that I wasn't engrossed in the daily tasks of mothering and homeschooling. That instead of the confident, smiling, put-together woman that I tried to project, I told them I felt small and confused.

No more "Linda is fine."

Can I just say how terrifying this was? Even with trusted friends? As they sipped their tea and nibbled on dessert, they continued to listen.

I found myself shaking as I blurted out my final question.

"How in the world do I do this next season of my life? I have no idea how to proceed."

Can you even guess what happened? The more vulnerable I was about my relational patterns, the more loved I felt by my friends. They were the definition of rock stars.

Each of them responded with a sober, "You too? I thought I was the only one! Perhaps we can help each other as we figure it out?"

I'd opened the door into a room that was new for us to sit in. Each of us began to share and cry and laugh and reassure each other that we weren't crazy. And we committed to stay intentionally vulnerable in this safe room we'd created. I'd never imaged how important it was to run alongside others through my life in a real and authentic way.

I'd run a couple of marathons in my late thirties rigorously training by running really long distances every week. Usually alone. Always carrying my own water. Wondering if I would find my way back home. Would I have enough energy? I was bored. Silenced. Yet determined.

Then came marathon day. What a contrast!

Surrounded by 20,000 other runners, I always had the opportunity to engage in friendly banter with someone. Volunteers handed me water without me even needing to ask for it. If I missed the handoff from one person, another was right there to fill in the gap. Mile markers showed me exactly where I was. No guessing on distance, hydration, or location. People covered me with cheers and encouragement giving me so much more fun than when I was training all alone.

In my life, I could choose to show my needs to others and grab the cups of water they offered. Or I could try to run the race all on my own. I could recognize the people in my life cheering for me or I could decide to go it alone on lonely dirt or concrete paths.

Isn't that the whole point? Together or alone? Avoidance and control OR connection and vulnerability?

It is all about our souls. How will we choose to live? How will I choose to live? That's the question.

BANGING MY HEAD

A robin pounding against the window echoed throughout the entire first floor of my house. What baffled me is that he did this to himself over and over and over. I simply couldn't understand it.

Unsuccessfully I tried to make him stop because I couldn't stand listening to this self-inflicted pain. I dashed outside to startle him. I pounded on the window from the inside to frighten him. But he only disappeared for a few minutes before he returned with increased vigor. Pounding away again.

My dad knew immediately why a robin would be hurting himself like this.

Dad explained that the robin saw a reflection of himself in the family room window and was simply protecting his territory. His focus was claiming our backyard as his. He thought he was fighting another male, but he was really fighting himself.

That was unbelievable to me.

"Even if it hurts him every time he crashes his head into the window?"

My dad nodded. "Yep," he said. "It's just like he'd battle another male robin. The pain is worth it."

So, with a new understanding, I watched this 'crazy' robin for a couple more days. I was astonished to notice a couple of things.

There were no other male robins anywhere in sight. None. He'd probably already cleared them away, but he was too focused on his own reflection to grasp the truth. And, literally two feet away from the family room window perched the female robin. She sat quietly on my flowerpot tilting her head up toward her lunatic lover as he kept intimidating his reflection in the window.

If only he would just turn around and see freedom from a threat and joy with his real prize. Oh, the pain he could prevent.

Playing in the background of my mind - during all this robin pounding - was a question of why it bothered me so much. After all, it was just a bird - and an ordinary one at that. Just an ordinary robin.

My dad's explanation gave me some clarity. The robin was fighting against himself. Unnecessarily.

Even though I'd come to recognize some areas in my life that needed to change, I've continued fighting against myself. Unnecessarily. For years. Here I thought I was simply processing the hurts that had accumulated in my heart. But I was replaying painful moments like somebody choosing to binge-watch Netflix.

Was I changing anything that had happened to me? No.

Was my pain lessening as I replayed the scenes? No.

Was I experiencing the freedom that I should be feeling in this season of my life? No.

I was just pounding again and again into those 'glassy' situations even though it was only hurting me and nobody else. Those poundings were distracting me from seeing the beauty around me. I was still guilty of focusing on parts of my life I couldn't control, but I realized that it was time to listen to fall.

It was time to die to the unhealthy belief that I could control things that I couldn't control.

It was time to die to the old lies and patterns that had been so deeply embedded in me.

It was time to die to what was hiding the healthy branches and stems from supporting my life.

It was time to remember that stupid robin banging his head against the window.

And it was time to become real. Finally.

JUST THREE QUESTIONS

I still remember the first time someone asked me this question.

"What do you want to be when you grow up?"

Without a moment of hesitation, I blurted, "Nothing. Just like my mom."

I was already well on my way to becoming a mom. After all, I'd diligently raised my baby doll, Thumbelina. After her 'birth' on Christmas Eve 1963, I tucked her into her cradle each night and scurried to greet her each morning. I really did. She accompanied me throughout my childhood and never made a peep. Please don't pop my bubble and tell me that was just because she was a doll.

But my answer to the most common question of all times ran deeper than my beloved Thumbelina. Who I wanted to be was standing right beside me.

I've often wondered what thoughts raced through Mom's mind when she heard I wanted to be 'nothing' just like her. Did she think I literally believed she was nothing? I confess that the words from the mouth of a six-year-old daughter could have stung. Fortunately, she never corrected or challenged me so my answer to that question remained the same for years.

I could never have articulated in those days what was underneath my answer, but somehow, I knew that in the truest parts of me, much of who I was, was reflected in my mom. Even at six years old.

We both loved to make music. To watch things grow. To be busy in the kitchen. To be surrounded by people. To encourage others. To punch out words on the typewriter.

Something about the unfiltered honesty of my little girl's answer still lingers in my heart and gives me clarity about moving forward as an adult.

Can I say, however, that it's a bit embarrassing to realize that slowly and steadily over time, I'd walked away from being the person that I thought I was created to be? That little girl who had a clear vision for who she wanted to be dissolved into a person that hid too much of her true self underneath the surface.

Can I also say that I feel some shame when I realize nobody ever asked me to tuck her away? In fact, I had people in my life who deeply encouraged me to thrive. But something in my spirit had grown afraid to fail, disappoint, or appear inadequate. I worked hard to control, not just my circumstances, but my emotions. Remember, I'd staked my claim to the great big four-letter word.

FINE.

Over time I began to care more about being liked and noticed and capable and fine than admitting I was vulnerable and scared and human. I was still banging my head against the window.

I got too good at covering me up. Until the gentle, and not so gentle, changes in my 'fine' life began to rub away at my heart like a fine-grit sandpaper.

Which brings me to the second question.

"What did you like to do when you were a little girl?"

My counselor's question came during a season where I was knee-deep unwrapping the plastic layers I'd wrapped around my heart. How in the world did she know that somewhere along the way, I'd lost some important parts of me? How did she know that when I was six years old, I'd been more in touch with 'me' than decades later?

I was skimming through life, doing good things, but not fully alive. I was distracted, hurried, and guarded. Yet I was working overtime to make sure everyone thought I was fine.

I was exhausted.

Most nights as I tried to fall asleep, I didn't feel like I'd done enough. Or that I wasn't enough. I was keeping score with some imaginary woman I'd created along the way, and 'she' was winning.

Remember, nobody asked me to become that other person. And I didn't wake up one morning deciding to do this to myself. I just slid into it ever so slowly without realizing it until one day I knew I couldn't 'do' life that way anymore. I needed to be me again.

I had to find the real Linda. Thus, the counselor's office.

Through our time together, we began to uncover many of my layers I'd accumulated during adulthood and begin to shine the light into my childhood. To how I spent my time when nobody demanded or expected anything from me.

"What did you like to do when you were a little girl?"

Ron's proposal of marriage was my most life-changing question. My counselor's insightful inquiry came in second.

Here's the list I blurted out quickly and passionately.

Knit and crochet

Work in the garden

Play the piano

Read book after book after book

Play outside in all seasons, especially at the crick

Ride my bike

Sew clothes for anybody who'd wear them

That was easy! I felt rather proud of myself for being so in touch with my childhood and the diversity of my interests.

But she wasn't done with me yet. Her third question proved to be more provocative and haunting.

"Which of those things are you doing now?"

Silence.

How in the world could I do any of those things now? Hadn't she heard me? I was way too busy doing things that were far more important than what I did when I was a little girl.

Hearing those words come out of my mouth caused me to shift uneasily on the leather upholstered chair. Intuitively I knew my thinking was flawed. In fact, Ron and I parented in hopes of encouraging our children to discover and live out who they were created to be. It was easy to identify parts of them that should always be expressed in their lives. Yet, I was guilty of not allowing myself to do the same.

I had to answer my counselor honestly.

"None of them," I sheepishly replied.

Silence.

Those three questions baked together to motivate me to begin a slow process of ripping out the lies I'd let myself believe so I could reveal my true self again. Just like unraveling row after row of a knitting project, I began to rip out the 'me' that God had not asked me to be or do.

This ripping out disappointed some because they heard me saying 'no' for the first time. It exposed my sensitive heart to others and for some, that was uncomfortable. But it also awakened parts of me that had been dormant for decades. In my newly awakening and empty spaces, I was able to be filled up with the truth about me again.

It didn't happen overnight. But it began to happen.

I've stopped apologizing when I pull out my latest knitting or crocheting project. Creating heirloom quality gifts for people that I love feels like a tangible, concrete way to encourage others. So, I found myself lingering at my local yarn shop literally breathing in the beauty of the multitude of textures and colors.

I began to garden with a whole heart. While some wince at the thought of digging in the dirt, I am wide awake and fully alive when my hands create beauty in the garden or my nose is buried in the scent of a freshly blooming flower.

In my 40's, I started taking piano lessons again and even played a Bach Fugue at a piano recital. It was so healthy for me to submit myself to teaching and making mistakes. But on the flip side, the music that was sleeping inside of me finally woke up. Becoming a piano student was one of the best decisions I made in that season.

And I started to read again. For pleasure. The rows of books on my bookshelves that I had reserved for 'someday' felt at home in my hands. I traveled to faraway places and times just by sitting on the front porch. As I read, I soared inside. And it ignited my desire to create with my own words again.

Recreation took on an entirely new meaning for me. I was literally re-creating me. It no longer felt like a waste of time to ride my bike. Or play my piano. Or read my book. Or plant my perennial. Such joy and freedom!

My fingers told the truth of my story as they caressed yarns, dug in the dirt, glided across the piano keys, and tentatively typed words that had been stored for years in my heart. Those fingers that had once been frozen began to move with agility and joy.

Most importantly, my heart that had been frozen began to see the lessons of each season in ways that words can't completely express. The changes occurring all around me had become the catalyst for changes to honestly occur within me.

So, I tenderly tiptoed into my life again.

UNDER CONSTRUCTION

I had determined at a young age that I was not going to marry a farmer or live in the country when I grew up. Influenced by television, I romanticized life in suburbia as portrayed by so many popular television shows of the '60s and '70s. Even though I was uncomfortable when I did leave the familiarity of my farming community, I was determined to find a way to fit in as a proper suburban woman. My head was filled with all the ways I should act in this very new way of life.

Part of my journey in reclaiming myself caused me to honestly embrace my farming roots. My husband and I decided to purchase a vacation home in rural Galena, IL. For nearly twenty years, this small-town environment literally helped recreate me.

People who know Ron and I well often believe this is where my husband healed from too many burdens on his very capable shoulders. And while they would be correct, my farmgirl spirit truly began to shine once again in this setting.

In this place, I found permission to listen to me again. Long walks or grueling runs on the rocky, hilly trail provided the space for the clutter in my heart to settle down. It was somewhere on that 17-mile trail that I got the courage to look for Linda again.

Slowly but surely, our weekends at the lake helped the image I wanted to see in my mirror become clear again. I was graciously accepted by my family as I communicated my need to embrace the country again. They watched me walk outside without shoes so I could feel life beneath my feet. They listened to my memories as the crops along Galena roads took me home to my roots. They explored the woods, collected wildflowers, and played at the beach with me. They found morel mushrooms and together we filled buckets with wild blackberries. They smiled when I raced outside to listen to the cattle mooing through the country air. They walked in the moonlight with me while the snow fell. Oh, the powerful hush in my heart.

My family was basically just about perfect for helping me become real.

This place provided the background for us to not just love each other, but to know and accept ourselves and each other.

No internet, cable, or phones. Just real-time conversation with the people I love more than any others in the world. Even though we carried a bit of the lake house rhythms back to suburbia with us, Ron and I grieved a bit every time we had to return to suburban life.

For Father's Day one year, I gave Ron a hammock to nestle in our backyard. It hung between two trees and held each of us as we cuddled, read, or watched the shooting stars. Until a deer tangled up in the rope and destroyed it. When we took the hammock down, we were stunned to see that the tree had grown around the supporting ropes leaving a mark of its presence in the bark.

This little yellow house in the hills of Galena helped rebuild me. Even with the best of intentions, I'd forgotten and buried who I was. While I thought I was soaking in the life of our family in that special place, my entire life has changed. The mark left upon my heart remains just like the mark of the rope wrapped around the tree

BRAVE NUMBER EIGHT

From the time he was a little guy, Jordan held a ball in his hand. Ron and I taught him right and left by pointing to his ball hand (right) and his glove hand (left). He entertained us for hours by dashing to his little toy chest to find whatever sporting gear would match the sport we were watching on TV. It didn't matter what it was. If tennis was on, he pretended to serve with his Nerf racket and ball. If football was on, he donned a little red helmet and grabbed his vinyl football. When the Chicago Cubs were playing, he quickly attached his Velcro laden glove and ball to his hand.

Sports were part of Jordan's core even at a young age. He was never content to just sit and watch. Playing a game of 'whatever sport' was just a different ball away.

Imagine my delight when Jordan contacted his future college's football coach to see if there were any spots left on the football team. Ron had suggested he try. And Jordan was all over it.

He had never played organized football!

Fortunately, his college team needed some players. When he transferred to Trinity International University in his junior year of college, he was finally able to put on a real uniform, pads, helmet, and cleats. I'll never forget the look of sheer, childlike delight when he approached his athletic locker for the first time. He was number eight.

I loved watching him on the sidelines of the games and wondered how many times he had imagined being on the field in uniform. The special team unit became extra special to my mother's heart as he walked on the field to block the opponent's field goal attempts.

What an honor to cheer from the sidelines for someone who had the courage to live out a dream!

When Jordan returned to college for his senior year, he had high hopes for a starting position on the football team. He suspected he had a chance to play quarterback, and he'd trained diligently all summer. But lots of new players had joined the team. Too many were experienced quarterbacks and fit Trinity's game plan better. So, while still working with the quarterbacks, he had to switch gears to find another way to contribute to his team. He fought for the kicking position. Despite a sore quad muscle and very little kicking practice, he pursued this job with the same enthusiasm he had as a little guy when we changed the television channel from one sport to another.

When I heard that he had lost the spot for starting kicker in a sudden death kicking competition, I felt like I'd been kicked in the stomach. Not only was I disappointed for him, I wanted to protect him from disappointment as well. Obviously, he was bummed. He wanted to play as much as possible in his senior year, and he wanted to know how he could tangibly contribute to his team. The season was still young, and my heart desperately hoped he would get to play so much that he would be completely worn out by the end of the season.

As I wrote earlier, I'm honestly ok that I didn't major in music. But I hate the reason why I didn't run after my dream. Watching Jordan fearlessly pursue something that may have been outside of his reach spoke quite loudly to me.

I missed out. Not just in participating in college music. I missed out on learning that facing disappointment is far better than harboring regrets. Now I watched my son and was inspired by seeing him model firsthand the joy that comes from avoiding regrets.

Trinity was clearly the underdog in the first game of the season. They were on the road, so we needed to wait for Jordan to call us to relay the final score. Sure enough, the sound of his voice told me the entire story. Or should I say his lack of voice?

He was completely hoarse from shouting and cheering from the sidelines. Did you catch that? Yes. From the sidelines. He made sure he had enough voice left in him should he be asked to step in as quarterback and call the plays on the field. But he didn't get to. Yet.

Disappointment sure. Regrets no. You see, he was on the team, and he was on the field. He was ready should he be needed. Once again, he was just an ask away. Way to go, Jordan!

Isn't that what fall is all about? Ready to give it all? To reap all that had been practiced and sown in the earlier seasons? I was so motivated to live with this reality that I began to believe I could handle disappointments. That was so much more palpable than living with regrets! Thank you, number eight!

SONGBIRDS AND STUFF

When Ron and I found out we were having a little girl, we agonized over her name more than we should have. We wanted our future daughter to grow up to be a strong woman with a clear voice that she recognized and used as her own. Even though I was still muddy in my own voice, I wanted our children to know their voices. Whether they were a son or a daughter.

Songbirds serenade me during my morning ventures into the woods and fill my backyard with song much of the year. I could visually recognize many species, but I also wanted to learn the unique songs of the birds that lived near me. I even learned how to caw a mean crow CAAWWW! But I also learned something much more significant than that.

Every species of bird sings unique songs. It seems obvious, but the truth of it never ceases to amaze me. A bird is completely content with the song that God has given it to sing, and unless it is a mockingbird, it wouldn't dream of imitating any other bird. The chickadee shrill cries out its name. Always. A robin sings like a robin. Always. The haunting coo of the mourning dove is balanced with the proud proclamation of the cardinals. Always.

I don't even have to look toward the sky anymore to know what bird is serenading me. Its songs are recognizable. Ron and I wanted to create an environment where our children could learn and sing the unique songs God gave them. Who wouldn't love to release a child into the world knowing he or she can sing the truth?

From the time Debralyn was born, music was her soothing comfort. Nothing calmed her down more quickly than an impromptu song from my lips. The very first night she slept in our home I sang to her as we waltzed around the living room.

She learned how to spell her name to the tune of *Twinkle, Twinkle, Little Star*. She even learned the sounds of the alphabet by singing. We created jingles for almost everything. Her desire to play the piano eloquently was in large part prompted by her desire to be able to accompany herself while she sang. It was no surprise when her nickname, Songbird Debralyn, stuck.

More importantly than music for this daughter of mine, however, is her desire to bring clarity and truth and healing to people she influences. She has sung this song locally and globally. Even before she leaned into her life's work, I would recognize her voice anywhere.

That's awesome, right? But I also knew that my daughter needed more.

She needed her mom to learn her own song too.

She needed me to learn how to embrace change without needing to tighten my control.

It was easy to 'control' young children.

It was even easier to 'control' their stuff. They complied with my requests to pick up their toys or to clean up their rooms. We gathered it, moved it, sorted it, and stored it. We used it, lost it, and replaced it.

You may wonder how all of this connects to learning how to sing my own song.

I'm honestly most content when all our stuff is in order and when I know where everything is. I relish an orderly home, organized bookshelves, and a predetermined place for all things that are ours.

As my children grew, I began to get a pit in my stomach when some of their stuff headed off to college with them. When the bridal shower and wedding gifts began appearing at my front door. When childhood boxes of memories disappeared into the depths of our crawl space. When I painted and redecorated kids' bedrooms to convert them to guest rooms and offices. Something felt so wrong with these changes.

I couldn't control the passing of time and my children's launching from the nest I had helped build for them. I had to admit that I still wanted to be the mother bird who was building her nest with sticks and leaves and mud rather than perching on the nest watching each of the baby birds fly out.

Yes. Here it is again. Control.

The tension between singing my song while watching their stuff disappear was real.

But if I was going to learn to sing my true song, I had to come to grips with the fact that my attachment to all this 'stuff controlling' represented painful emotions buried beneath the surface.

My 'emotional stuff' mirrored the 'physical stuff' that was out of my control. I was cluttered, scattered, and unsettled. I couldn't find my footing in this unfamiliar territory. I wanted to be able to simply pick everything up, put it in order, and feel fine.

But that would have been just like a cardinal singing a robin's song.

As I watched Jordan and his bride, Jacqui, load up all his/her/their stuff and move into their first home, I was inspired. For months, their stuff had been scattered at college, our home, and her family home in Missouri. But soon it would be all in one place.

Who doesn't love watching newlyweds set up their first home? They don't know where everything will go yet or how the darling apartment will look when they are done. But they are 'at it.' They aren't avoiding the work of settling their stuff just because they don't know the end of their story.

Could the same be said of unpacking and settling into my emotional world? I can't control the end of my story, but I can control being real and authentic even if I'm messy sometimes.

Emotional ping-pong is far healthier than emotional numbness.

Part of my song includes the melody of being able to hold more than one emotion at one time. It's ok to celebrate the great young adults my children have become. And it's also ok to miss doing day to day life with them in my home.

Graduations. Weddings. Joyous occasions. U-Hauls. Empty closets. Yuck.

Change. I can unpack my emotional boxes one at a time. Almost like Jordan and Jacqui unpack their boxes. They may finish first, but that's ok. It's not a race. I can embrace doing the things that I need to do to sing my real song. Vulnerable conversations with family and friends. Playing Bach on the piano. Long runs in the woods. Lingering in my garden. The more I do this, the more beautiful I will sing.

CLEARING OUT OVERGROWTH

I've decided that farmers actually have it right. When they plant their crops each spring, they wisely adjust the settings on the planter to space the seeds appropriately. They know the right space needed for proper growth and development of their crops that they anticipate harvesting in the fall.

If they're like me, they may have had at least one year when they erred a bit on the 'thick' side. And regretted it so, they adjusted and set it all straight.

When I set out to create a luscious perennial garden in my backyard, I honestly didn't want it to look bare and boring as it was establishing itself. Even though every book I read on the topic suggested a proper spacing amount, I talked myself into believing I knew better.

For example, if the 'expert' recommended planting with 18" of space between each perennial, I decided I'd like my results far better if I planted them about 10" apart. And for the first couple of years, I was pretty proud of my gardening savvy.

Then the next year, plants stopped blooming. Some stopped growing. Others had disappeared altogether. Their roots had grown so thickly that they literally couldn't get the nutrition and water they needed to live. Unless I divided them and followed the spacing wisdom, they would never thrive.

The truth about me is that I would much rather plant and create than divide and redo. It's one thing to spend my springtime afternoons optimistically planting perennials (albeit too close together) than to spend my autumn afternoons digging and dividing. That feels a bit defeating. I no longer feel like I am nurturing new growth. Instead, I'm being rough and ruthless to salvage the results of my foolishness. Apparently, I am skeptical of whether dividing plants will make any difference or not.

I leaned into the wisdom of creating spaces. Of giving each plant enough room to do what it was made to do. It became a sort of a challenge.

I found myself holding my coffee mug while gazing critically to decide what changes must be made before the winter chills arrived. What plants needed to be moved? To be divided. To be cut back. Where do I want the space to plant bulbs this fall, yet leave room to plant annuals next spring? What risks are worth taking?

I've got lots to learn from the autumn work of dividing and moving and creating spaces.

In the 'olden' days of paper calendars and voice messaging machines, I felt much more important and needed if my calendar was full of tasks, appointments, and activities for my kids. While I winced when there were too many voice messages on my answering machine when I got home from another 'out and about' I felt a little forgotten if there were no messages.

If I saw an outfit I liked, I wanted to buy it. And I often did. My closet stash grew and grew and grew as I was chasing the illusion of fitting in and receiving the affirmation that I thought I needed.

I liked a full refrigerator, freezer, and bookcase. I accumulated far too much. And for the wrong reasons. I was using the 'next new thing' to help me avoid feeling whatever I should have been feeling.

I wasn't sure what the right amount to accumulate was, but I knew that having too much was distracting me from the truth about my life. Once again, my family became my inspiration to realize that stuff didn't matter nearly as much as moments did.

I was in the basement when my youngest son, Josh, hollered urgently to me from the kitchen.

"Mom! Mom!! Mom!!! Come up here. Hurry!"

To be honest, I was more than a bit annoyed to be interrupted in doing my 'whatever'. Ah, that important task. So important that I can't even remember what I was doing when I look back now. But I clearly remember what Josh had waiting for me.

A moment.

I reluctantly trudged up the stairs only to find Josh standing by the patio window staring west toward the sunset.

The western sky glowed with so many vivid shades of violet, pink, orange, and gold. It was as if a master artist had thrown every gorgeous color into the sky and it stuck.

The silhouettes of the newly barren trees only highlighted the breathtaking beauty.

"Mom, we've waited all summer to finally see the sunsets again. Right?" He knew that the dense woods behind our home blocked the summer sunsets. I had told him for months to just wait. I'd promised that the sunsets would burst through the empty spaces once the leaves had fallen to the ground.

I had told him to be ready once the 'fullness of summer' had disappeared. But I was still so caught up in my 'tasks' and my 'stuff' that I could have missed it all if it weren't for his 10-year-old eyes and uncluttered heart.

"Oh dear, Josh, you are so right." Once again, my family had become my teacher.

Without Josh, I would have missed it. Without fall, I would miss so much. When's the last time you really looked at a sunset? The vivid and emptier spaces created during fall beg with inviting voices to see what's on the other side of the trees.

I'll always be grateful to Josh to bring me out of the depths of the 'basement' to see fall's luscious sunset.

Life is so full. Summer's landscape is so full.

We need the shedding of fall to see the beauty that is behind the luscious green of summer.

We need the dividing work of fall to create spaces to experience the most beautiful parts of life.

This shedding looks different for each of us. But part of it for me was learning to let go of how I used a full calendar and full closet to try to paint an image of me that was a lie. No more putting on the show even though I'd gotten good at it.

It's my journey that continues even today, but I can attest to the freedom I feel in the spaces I've created by not filling up everything in my garden and in my life.

I can attest to wisely waiting through the silences of the winter and early rains of spring. I can wait as I welcome the green tips of my bulbs that now have room to grow and perennials that look alive again.

I can feel the freedom of not needing to use my 'busyness' to create an illusion of my importance. I can embrace the joy of letting go of the stuff that distracts me from seeing the sunsets.

Thank you, Josh.

PRELUDES AND FUGUES

Johanne Sebastian Bach has always been my favorite composer. But during my growing up years, I never dreamed of playing one of his more challenging compositions. Remember, I was afraid to fail at anything. So, I played it safe. Literally. By playing the music that I'd heard before and that didn't require my fingers to be quite so agile. I was at home in the comfort zone.

When I bravely began taking music lessons again in my 40's, my persistent and perceptive teacher, Marilyn, handed me a book of Bach's preludes and fugues. Apparently, she thought it was her duty to make sure I tackled at least one of them. After communicating all the reassurances that she could muster, I headed home and sat down on my piano bench. I opened my new and intimidating golden-colored book.

Slowly but surely, I began pounding out the theme Bach had written with my right hand. My tempo was slow, and my heart was pounding in step with his theme. Something instantly ignited a spark inside of me. The place in my stomach that normally aches during sad good-byes was now fluttering with butterflies.

And I kept going. Adding my left hand to the mix (after practicing on its own, of course) literally created tears in my eyes. I couldn't help but notice that the theme was tucked inside of what my left hand was playing as well. Brilliant work, Mr. Bach. The theme repeated itself in both of my hands. My responsibility was to simply notice it and let it shine.

I practiced and practiced and practiced. I worked so hard to pull out the theme whether it was played with my right hand or my left. When the key changed from major to minor, I kept going. I was searching for the theme in my heart and did all that I could do to highlight it when I played.

I timidly performed my Bach piece for my teacher at my next lesson. Then I took a risk.

"I think I was created to play Bach."

I didn't know what Marilyn would say. After all, she'd taught the best of the best. She was beyond the best of the best music teachers in my geographical area. I was just a 40 something mother facing her empty nest who longed to keep the sound of music alive in her home. Who was I to think I should focus on playing Bach? Remember, I was the one who bailed on studying music in college?

Without a moment of hesitation, she cheerfully said, "Well, let's go then!" In a flash, she scurried to her music shelves to grab all the Bach books her tiny frame could carry.

Oh, the power of someone believing in me!

As long as I continued to take piano lessons from Marilyn, she had a continuous fountain of music from Mr. Bach for me to embrace. As only she could do, she almost made me believe he had written them just for me so I could play my heart out on the keys of her baby grand piano.

And here's why this is so important.

Musically, I learned to recognize repeated themes. Mr. Bach was the king of finding unique ways to repeat a theme in his music, not only in the right hand versus left hand but in key and tempo changes. And in far more ways than I can even articulate.

Somewhere during all this Bach playing, I realized that I had some similar themes playing over and over in my life. People I dearly loved continued to die. The best of friends moved to different time zones. Each child getting closer to leaving this wonderful nest Ron and I had given our best to create. The theme of letting go.

But the most vivid of all this 'theme repetition' was what I witnessed first-hand in my dad. My dad never knew how to play the piano or how to critically analyze a piece of classical music. Yet, he recognized the beauty of listening to the music coming from my fingers.

"Play it again, Sam," Dad pleaded. He knew that my days of living on the farm with Mom and him were nearing an end. It took me nearly forty years for me to walk in his shoes. To understand his vantage point. To hear 'Bach's' theme of change repeating year after year.

Another trip around the sun. Another fall and harvest season. Do that forty more times.

My ninety-six-year-old dad now needs his walker or wheelchair to make his way through his home. He used to attack the harvest with strength and passion and energy. He now watches his younger neighbors, brother, and nephew from the uncomfortable comfort of his living room recliner. He has let go of so much. That seems to be the theme he's repeating these days.

When Dad began to wonder where his wagons were in late August, it dawned on me. He was used to the theme of harvest each fall. He was exactly on time realizing that he needed to have his wagons at the ready.

He knew it was fall and time to harvest. He was confused this year about what that meant. But he did know that if he was going to harvest his field corn, he needed his wagons.

I was heartbroken. I could still see my strong and capable dad marching through our yard heading toward the combine. I could still see him pulling his wagon behind the tractor and alongside the combine so that he captured every single ear of corn that should end up in the crib.

"Where are my wagons?" he asked repeatedly.

He hasn't used wagons for decades, but the familiar themes of fall told him it was time to find the wagons.

The light. The shadows. The ripening grains. Play it hands alone or hands together on the piano. It doesn't matter. It's fall. Dad's right.

He needed his wagons.

So, I dug through my photo albums that I had created years ago. I wanted him to see his wagon that had once been essential to the fall. I also wanted him to see that he didn't need them anymore.

In a simple 3-ring binder, Dad saw copies of his wagon that he desperately needed in the 1970's. He also looked at pictures of the newer combine that replaced his need for that wagon in the 1980's. I also hope that he felt honored and treasured and embraced for his ability to see beyond the wagons and combines and corn.

The familiar and repeated theme of harvest, which had been a part of his life for over 90 years, was crystal clear in his heart. After playing it for decades, why should this year be any different?

I heard my dad play a different theme this year. Perhaps the key was minor and the tempo slower. But no matter. It still sounded like harvest. And it was ferociously beautiful.

When change occurs, it's human nature to dig around for something familiar. Even if that wasn't what Bach set out to do, it's how I experienced his musical feats. My dad, as he nears his last seasons, recognized a longing for his familiar wagons. But this phenomenon doesn't only happen toward the end of our lives.

Debralyn sent me this Facebook message.

"Ok. Not gonna lie. Watching NBC cover the royal wedding this morning has me wishing I could wake up early and grab some coffee and sit on the couch with you and be ridiculously girly for a couple of hours."

Debralyn had just graduated from a rigorous master's program. Wrote a thesis. Lived on adrenaline to survive and finish. When her life calmed down, something triggered a desire for a familiar theme. She wasn't searching for long lost wagons, but she was searching for long ago carefree summer days when she and I giggled and spent hours doing all things 'girly.' We still acknowledge that theme for both of us, but it sounds different these days. It sounded beautiful then, and it sounds beautiful now. Just different. And we are learning how to embrace the changes of key and tempo while we continue to play familiar themes in new ways.

COMPLETELY TORN OUT

Tearing down our swimming pool felt like someone was amputating my arm.

Ron and I never would have built a swimming pool in our backyard, but since the perfect home for us happened to have one, we went with it. I am definitely not a swimmer, but fortunately, this pool had a large deck surrounding it, so I didn't have to 'suffer' in the water unless I chose to.

Yet for our family, summer equaled pool and pool equaled summer. We drank far too many lemon spritzers. We licked far too many ice cream bars. We spent too many hours playing with friends. We laughed and played and swam too much.

Or did we? It was summer after all.

And then it was time for it all to be over. And I had this sickening sensation that tearing down our pool would be only the first domino of change. One would fall after the other in increasingly rapid succession. If we didn't rip out the pool, could that stop the other changes from happening?

As I stood on the deck which surrounded the 'now needing expensive repair' pool, I still heard the screeches of my little kiddos and their friends splashing and shouting 'Marco Polo!' I heard my husband and children playing pool basketball acting like their very lives depended on each and every basket.

Yet, the time had come to create something new. Playing in a 4 ft. deep pool as little kids was awesome. But as a family of full-grown people, we had outgrown this space. The ripped liner and sagging deck demanded an answer.

In Ron's typical wisdom, he saw a future for our backyard that would embrace me. A garden. A writer's garden as he called it. How could he envision a future while I kept holding onto the past?

I don't like change. And I don't like that change is inevitable. And you know what? I usually want to go back to the way things were or fast forward to the future after the dust of change has settled. It's the in-between that is pretty unsettling.

Not this time. I was determined to put into practice the work that I've been doing to be real and handle even the simplest of changes with authenticity.

It's a good thing I had done some of that work because when the demolition crew showed up, my face still looked rather dismayed. So, dismayed in fact that they walked away when they saw the tears flowing down my cheeks. I was so sad that Ron even offered to call the whole pool tearing out thing off.

But I wasn't just crying about a pool.

I was crying because I couldn't remember the exact moment we sat dripping on the chairs by this pool for the last time. Were we all there? Had we paused to wonder if this would be the last time? Or had we just routinely closed the pool last fall assuming we'd open it again in the spring just like we'd done for so many years.

How many times have I lived through the last time without knowing it was the last time? That question tormented me until the demolition crew brought me back to reality.

Our summertime pool and its surrounding deck came down bit by bit. The liner, the stabilizers, the decking pieces, and the filters were laid out for all to see in our driveway.

When the demolition crew pulled away, I didn't even recognize my backyard. For nearly twenty years, my view toward the west had been overshadowed with the protective wall of a deck and pool. Now our backyard had a gaping, ugly hole. And unlike the hole left by a lost baby tooth, nothing new was poised and ready to fill its place. Its absence created a visual void that I wasn't sure I knew how to fill. Did I even want to fill it?

I must be honest. I wasn't grieving the loss of my pool. I was grieving all that this summertime, childhood fun pool represented. The changes ahead for our family would be more dramatic and more accelerated than in the past. I wasn't prepared to embrace the fact that I couldn't rewind or stop it or even slow it the clock. Tick tock. Tick tock.

The pool had taken on more than it was. It was the symbol of everything that I had loved about this sweet summertime season in our family. I didn't want anything to change. With or without a pool.

I'll forever be grateful for Ron's words as he predicted my struggles in this transition. He encouraged me to create a flower garden in the void that was once filled with a pool. Was he also suggesting that I could begin to write in the empty spaces that were no longer being filled with my homeschooling responsibilities?

That was so hard to embrace. I'd loved every season of mothering. I don't remember complaining about the infant, toddler, child, or even adolescent years we experienced with our sons and daughter. But I was beginning to complain in my spirit. I wanted to hold onto my family of five living under our roof, yet I didn't want to stop my children from living the lives they were created to live.

"A writer's garden," he had said. In those three words, Ron gently reminded me that I was made to dig in the dirt and use words to capture what I noticed in creation.

I had to admit he was right.

Once the pool was removed and new sod was laid, my courage and creativity took over. Honestly, I was convinced that I could create a medley of perennial colors. My father's farming spirit and mother's nurturing soul had formed my love of beauty in the out-of-doors. These empty spaces were begging to be filled. I could either ignore or embrace the chance to be Linda. I'd fought too hard to reclaim 'her' so I admitted that I was more comfortable digging in the dirt than floating in the chlorinated pool.

The metaphorical season of fall helped me reclaim the last bits of myself that I had tucked away. So, grabbing my fears and insecurities by their sticky little fingers, I invited them to join me as I began to plan and dream. With a few gardening books, blank sheets of paper, and colored pencils, I grabbed my lawn chair and planted myself in the middle of the 'pool'. It was time to create.

Meandering through my local garden center, I found myself finding comfort in the zinnias. I was drawn to them and felt like a little girl again in my grandma's garden. Row after row of colorful zinnias danced in the breeze all summer until the late fall frost unless they were gathered for a miniature vase placed on her kitchen table.

I'd fallen in love with gardening when my mom let me water our zinnias every night after supper. As soon as I was strong enough, I filled a pail at the water pump and used a discarded soup can to make sure these gorgeous flowers would flourish. I can still see the black dirt drink up the water as I nurtured these garden plants. Watering the zinnias was never a chore. Yet, I had seen them as ordinary and expected. I had no idea that one day they would be just what I needed to help me through one transition after another.

So, as I plotted out spots for all the perennials to bloom throughout the spring, summer, and fall, I made sure there'd always be a spot for my zinnias.

Zinnias. The familiar flourishing amongst the new. Perhaps that is how I will survive the fall season that now defines my family.

PART III

But the little Rabbit sat quite still for a moment and never moved. For when he saw all the wild rabbits dancing around him, he remembered his hind legs...He actually had hind legs! Instead of dingy velveteen, he had brown fur, soft and shiny, his ears twitched by themselves, and his whiskers were so long that they brushed the grass.

He gave one leap and the joy of using those hind legs was so great that he went springing about the turf on them, jumping sideways and whirling about as the others did.

He was a Real Rabbit at last, at home with the other rabbits.

The Velveteen Rabbit

FINDING PENNIES

Annie Dillard wrote about her childhood mischief in *Pilgrim at Tinker Creek*. As a little girl, she loved drawing arrows in chalk pointing to a mysterious destination with the words, "Surprise ahead! Don't miss it!" When the occasional pedestrians discovered her scribbled words, they were on the brink of a miracle. An often-overlooked copper-colored penny tucked in a crack of the concrete was waiting to change everything for them.

Imagine her childlike delight as she hid to watch others discover the miracle of a free penny! Every time I read that section in her book, I find myself hoping people smiled and whooped with delight at her exuberance over a mere penny.

But here's the point.

Pennies are literally spread throughout the world. No, they aren't made of copper. And they aren't highlighted with chalk arrows or billboard signs. But they are there. They just need me to open my eyes wide enough to see them.

Through this becoming real and seeking to joyfully embrace the changes in my life, I intuitively knew that part of my journey needed to include a spirit of gratitude. Whether it was only measured as the value of a penny or worth thousands of dollars. No matter what change blew in the wind, there must be something to be grateful for. Could it be true that we can seize copper penny gratitude if we simply open our eyes to see?

There it was. Right in front of me. Tucked in a crack in the sidewalk. Part of the secret to all of my desire to be able to dance with joy is to offer thanks for what has been and for what's to come.

Few places demonstrate that as concretely as my backyard garden each fall when I tuck it in for its long winter's nap. My summer blooms have outdone themselves displaying their glorious colors, but now they've sadly turned brown and crunchy after the first frost of the season. Rainy, cloudy weather usually sets in so I must grab this tiny window of opportunity to work before winter arrives.

With layers of grayish clouds covering the sky and dipping temperatures, my feet crunch over the colorful leaves that carpet the ground.

It's so easy to soak in the pennies that surround all my senses as I begin dividing, pruning, and yanking. Yes. I am thankful for what has been. My garden, of its own accord, outdoes itself with continuous beauty all spring and summer long. But it is time to let it take its winter nap.

I have a confession to make.

Springtime gardening is much easier. Growth is right around the corner and results tangibly show themselves after the first warm rainfall. I can tiptoe outside anytime I want to see little green shoots of growth. It's easy to anticipate with gratitude what's to come. It's right there in front of me.

In the fall, however, I must be content. I do all this fall preparation only to enter into a season of waiting through the quiet, underground months of winter. Trying to be grateful for what's to come feels so much more difficult because I honestly don't know what will come after the icy, cold, blustery winter days.

Most falls, I've faithfully dug holes to the right depth and added the right amount of bone meal before I carefully planted dozens of tulip bulbs. I don't know if it was squirrels, voles, or bad planting, but none of them grew.

Should I be grateful for that? It doesn't feel like it. I hate wasted effort.

Every fall as I cut down my fearless zinnias, my fingers rub their brown and brittle faces to release dried seeds to the ground. My gardening friend has promised that those seeds will take root and grow next summer even though a zinnia doesn't survive the winter in Illinois.

Nothing. Never.

Yet year after year, I try, but my warnings grow louder.

"Why do I waste my money and energy on tulip bulbs? What am doing wrong?" I wonder.

"Beware of squirrels and rabbits and deer who love to eat plants. Should I rip them out?" My thoughts don't stop there.

Dorothy's lions and tigers and bears. Oh my.

"Don't plant so deep that they won't have the strength to grow and bloom."

"Don't plant so shallow that the frozen ground will heave them o the surface."

How do I look at the preparing and the waiting as an opportunity to find an obvious penny up ahead on the sidewalk?

More importantly, how can I incorporate the discipline of being grateful for what's to come when I have no idea what's to come?

The natural rhythms of the seasons display a more accurate mirror into who I am than the mirror that hangs in my bathroom. t's hard to wait and even harder to embrace gratitude when I prefer immediate gratification and feedback. And I do mean immediate.

That's what was mulling around in my heart as I tried for the ast time to plant tulip bulbs.

As I carefully tucked those little brown babies in the ground, I admitted that I hadn't known the future all along, even though I thought I was still in control. I'll plant and try to let it go. And try to be thankful?

During all this digging and planting, I remembered something profound I'd learned from my son, Josh, years ago.

Josh was born grateful. He said thank you to anyone and everyone for anything and everything.

When he was a little boy, he had a 'tell' at mealtime. Nobody taught him to do this, and it was utterly adorable. When we served him his plate of food, we knew right away if he thought he would like it or not.

If he suspected that this was a 'gag down and get through it' kind of meal, before he took one bite, he said, "Thank you." He expressed gratitude first because, in his logical young mind, he probably didn't think he'd want to say thank you for say, eggplant parmesan after he had to eat it.

So, he was grateful first.

If we served him a bowl of macaroni and cheese, he didn't say thank you until every luscious bite was safely stored in his tummy. He knew that 'thank you' would be easy before he even had a taste.

His gratitude went beyond mealtime. Josh approached the proctor before his ACT exam and thanked her for her presence. Who does that? This was not just a quirk. Gratitude was and is a part of how he is wired. Grateful. No matter what.

So as I once again began to plant the bulbs assuming they wouldn't grow either, I wondered how I could copy Josh.

What would it look like if I learned to say thank you for the future even without knowing what it would hold? Even if I was suspicious that I wouldn't like it? To be honest, Josh's gratitude for what he thought he wouldn't like meant more than his expressions of thanks for his favorite meals.

Be thankful for what has been and for what's to come. Regardless of what the future may 'taste' like.

In other words, take delight over a copper penny even if I had thought I'd find a thousand-dollar bill.

DAY BY DAY BY DAY

A few weeks ago, a friend honestly explained how she is thinking and feeling about her 'almost' empty nest. After she finished, she asked me a seemingly simple question.

"How have you handled your season of transition?"

You'd think I'd have no problem putting words around these past few years given the amount of time I've spent writing/thinking/feeling. Instead, I came up blank.

How in the world have I handled this season of transition?

I'd unsuccessfully crafted my response to this question so many times. I simply told her I'd have to think about it. That's Linda's code for I have no idea!

While so many parts of the past few years are vividly loud, much of my life has all blurred together. And the blur isn't because I was moving too fast – it is simply the nature of transition. One scene blurring into the next. And the next. And the next. And then suddenly, I am sitting here. I'm sitting in today.

I've had moments these past few years when I didn't think I could breathe as I let my children go. When I had no words to say when it was time to say good-bye to all that felt familiar. When I wanted to trade places with families with young children. When I wondered what the point of it all was anyway.

On the other hand, there were other times when I was so excited about the opportunities my children had. My heart was borderline bursting. When I saw them have the courage to fly, I raised my fist in the air to cheer them on.

So, my short answer to the big question is that I have learned, wait, I mean I'm trying to learn, to hold more than one kind of emotion at a time. It's not all one or the other like I thought it should be. Can I feel sadness and joy at the same time?

But my long answer to the big question dawned on me when I opened my backdoor to take another picture of my backyard.

One March I began taking a daily photo of my garden. I merely slid open the screen door, pointed my camera, and shot the photo. Then on a tiny slip of paper, I noted the date and time of date.

Day by day by day I paused for just a second and really saw what was literally staring at me outside my own backdoor.

For almost a year, I took a photo of my writer's garden, and here's my most valuable lesson.

All along, I'd thought that I was living in a season of transition for the first time. The truth was actually this.

I always have been and always will be living in a season of transition. All that varies is how subtle or how dramatic those transitions are.

So, it began in March.

"The end of winter approaches. Some feeble coverings of snow remain while the buds are beginning to awaken."

"Receding snow, even though the March night tipped the grass with frost. The air begins to warm in the morning sunlight."

"The dirt will soon be inviting more green shoots to grow. The sunset lingers just a bit longer these days. And one can never predict April weather. A crispy and frosty morning dawn, but the noontime sun warms."

Day by day by day.

"Blue skies. The wheel marks of freshly mowed grass. The garden fairies have arrived and touched their magic wands on the early summertime flowers."

"Without a bit of effort on my part, perennial stems inch their way toward the sky. Little lavender-colored lilac buds open to fill my soul with the scent of heaven. Inhale. Breathe it in."

"As not to be outdone, the roses appear. They are just the right height to whisper their joy. Each day brings a bit more fullness of color and texture."

Winter is a distant memory. Was this place once covered in white?

"Everything is extra verdant after the morning shower."

"Another season has passed while another one arrives. The warmth radiates across the yard."

Did you catch it? As one daily scene fades into the next, the change isn't all that dramatic. But if you were to scroll back to the first image of my backyard and then fast forward to the last image, the changes between the two don't seem possible.

That's how it has been with my mother's heart. One day faded into the next over and over and over. I probably didn't truly notice all the subtle nuances until that big moment. Whatever big moment that was.

Finishing homeschooling. The last dinner around the kitchen table before leaving for college. A wedding shower. Waving good-bye to children traveling to Europe. Listening to my youngest son negotiate the purchase of my father's car. Meeting grandchildren. Adding more and more chairs to the kitchen table for the ones that now belong in our family.

These big season-marking moments will continue and for right now, they will probably come one right after the other. But, so will the subtle day by day moments that I don't want to miss if I'm only focusing on the big ones. In fact, one is probably right in front of me if I open my eyes.

These moments are all over the place.

Changes.

Big ones and subtle ones.

My backyard still invites me into its classroom as each day it teaches me about subtle changes that help prepare me for the big ones.

So, I no longer apologize for holding a mug of coffee as I start my day gazing into my garden. As I sip, I embrace. It is good. Day by day by day.

SURPRISED BY JOY

No matter how hard my brain works, I just don't get some things.

I don't get how there are some intersections where I swear I've never hit a green light yet regardless of the direction I'm driving. Wouldn't you think I'd have at least a tiny chance of getting a green light sometimes?

And I certainly don't get expressway traffic jams. Unless there is an accident or a blizzard, I don't understand how my speed fluctuates between 0mph and 50mph within seconds. Somebody or something has to be at the front right? Yet, I've never seen him, her, or it.

And, please, please, please don't ask me how the moon 'works'. Even though I taught my three children about the solar system year after year, I still am confused every time I try to figure out the phases of the moon. I don't get it. Give me a darkened bathroom, a flashlight, baseball, and ping pong ball, I've got it. Put me outside under the magical moonlit sky, and I am utterly clueless. The moon is a miracle that I don't understand.

At a deeper level, there are other things I don't get.

Why does seeing a stained-glass window transport me back to my childhood Vacation Bible School? Why am I suddenly a little girl gluing red translucent strips of plastic over the holes cut in black construction paper? No matter how hard I try, I can't create any more of that picture.

I chase after more, and while it's almost there, I can't quite grasp onto it.

I wonder why I can't listen to some pieces of classical music without stopping in my tracks. Tears welling in my eyes. Waves of unnamed emotions bubbling almost to the surface.

Why do I stop everything when I hear a deep wind roaring through the newly barren forest trees? I've heard that sound somewhere before and I can almost, and I mean almost, find where my heart is trying to take me.

Is it somewhere like home?

My list could go on – there are far too many things that I just don't get.

But maybe, just maybe, I'm beginning to put some of the pieces together.

It starts with those deep in the gut feelings that suddenly burst to the surface and then quickly dive underground. It's like seeing a lightning bug, but when we try to catch it where it last lit up, it's gone. Fleeting. We are convinced we just saw it beckoning us to grab it. But then it darkened only to light up somewhere else. The chase and catch game continues until we either catch it or until we decide to wait for another night.

The deep in my gut feeling came when I rocked my grandson, Carter, to sleep on an old, forgotten, yet familiar rocking chair. Because I'd recently read *Surprised by Joy* by C.S. Lewis, I felt like I had a clue as to what it was all about. He reminded me that joy wasn't in my control. Pleasure possibly was, but joy came in unexpected and inexplicable fleeting moments. Those moments could have originated in our childhood and later got lost as we grew.

As I rocked my young grandson, Carter, my feeling was one of desire and longing, but it had nothing to do with the moment of rocking him in the chair. It had everything to do with the fact that this chair was a chair I hadn't seen for decades but was probably the first wooden rocker I remembered. While I rocked Carter, my

116

heart replayed a vignette of images creating joy. That 'surprised by joy' kind of joy.

I had to have been barely three years old when Grandma rocked me on her lap as we sat on her simple, sparse, and sacred sun porch.

Every wooden item was painted gray except that rocking chair. Most of the time we sat side by side in a large wicker chair, but not this day. It was a day I asked Grandma to hold and rock me. On the same chair where I was rocking Carter.

As she held and rocked, she read her sparse collection of children's books over and over. For every book she read, I tried to imagine that I was one of the main characters in the book. All while rocking and riding through the stories on my grandma's lap.

After I was thoroughly satisfied that I had 'ridden' enough, I declared that it was time to color.

"Let's only use orange today," I announced. Even though orange was a strange color to pick for this blue loving girl, Grandma wholeheartedly agreed. Still rocking, we each grabbed an orange crayon and began to color our way through her one and only coloring book. We giggled as little faces of children and puppies turned orange.

The sounds of that wooden rocker rubbing against the gray wooden planks stopped. It is my last memory of rocking in that simple sunroom on my grandma's lap.

I can't find anymore. No matter how hard I tried to remember as I gazed into Carter's dreamy face, my memory faded. Just like the lightning bug. I was back in the here and now. Rocking and holding. Yet somehow more anchored in my life.

I don't get how a simple, old rocking chair could surprise me with joy. Yet it did. As mysterious as the lunar phases of the moon, this magical chair surprisingly cried out with joy.

Is that part of the secret of embracing joy when changes abound? Is it learning to hold familiar emotions even when the original root feels hidden behind a veil? Is it understanding how to be quiet and slow enough to notice when our heart begs asks us to listen? To feel joy? Even if we don't get it?

Perhaps.

THE HIGHWAY OR THE WOODS

I was wide awake at 3 am. For literally no explainable reason. I wasn't sick. I wasn't cold. I wasn't hot. I wasn't hungry. And I certainly wasn't tired.

So, I lay there. Reminding myself that I needed to add avocados to my grocery list. That I needed to start a load of laundry as soon as I got up. Deciding whether to run first and then get ready for my day or go to the grocery store first, then run, and then get ready for my day. Yada, yada, yada. You know. Those critical 3 am decisions.

Then I reminded myself to add kitchen garbage bags to my current unwritten grocery list. Don't forget to finish my blog on hospitality. And my poor little flowers need watering as soon as possible. Should I start knitting that aqua vest or the little sweater next?

Do. Do. Do. Do. Do. Do. Each 'do' was getting louder than the last one.

Thoughts bounced around and bombarded my mind. I should be sleeping. I've got so much to do when I wake up.

If I wake up.

BecausewhatifIdon'tfallbackasleepbeforethealarmgoesoff?

I think you get the idea.

I've had nights when I've been too worried or too excited or too afraid to sleep. I've used the dark hours of the night to pray or sift through my burdens. Those sleepless hours seemed valuable and justifiable.

But this private nighttime conversation wasn't so noble. I was just awake obsessing about an unwritten, silly old to-do list. Yep. I am like Winnie the Pooh, that silly old bear.

Unfortunately, I didn't go back to sleep.

So, when the alarm finally gave me permission to put an end to that nonsense, I made an extra-strong pot of coffee, threw in a load of laundry, added avocados and kitchen garbage bags to my visible grocery list, and decided I was too tired to run. So, a walk it would be followed by a quick trip to the grocery store. Then my day could begin in earnest.

I literally had the next two hours of my life all figured out. Good job to me!

Just as I was about to head out for my walk, I felt a little nudge to grab my camera and put on my glasses. Maybe there'd be something special to see this morning?

As often happens when I place myself in creation, I discovered I needed to see more than what was in front of me. I needed to see what was brewing in me.

Under the fading moon and the rising sun, I began to inhale. My mind slowed down as I noticed the wooded path leaning into all the beauty that the season of fall had to offer. The mature milkweed pods were overflowing with white tufts of fluff gently swaying in the chilly breeze. The fallen leaves crunched under my feet to accompany the songs of the few birds that hadn't yet begun their southern migration. Clump after clump of golden and russet-colored prairie grasses waved good morning. Yes, a new and glorious day was right in front of me.

By the time I had turned around to head home, my mental to-do list was gently recalibrating.

I only need avocados because everyone's coming home this weekend, and we're making homemade sushi together. With avocados.

I only need to start a load of laundry because my running clothes smell after all the fun I've had running on my healthy legs in beautiful places.

I can go to the grocery store without any worries about how I'll pay for whatever I buy.

I have a bed to sleep or to not sleep in.

I have time to use my fingers to knit lovely gifts for others while enjoying the process of watching the stunning patterns of the yarns unfold right before my eyes.

By the time I needed to cross the highway from the woods back to my neighborhood, I was a wide-awake version of me again and ready to step into my day.

I couldn't help but notice a sharp contrast between the serenity and authenticity of the woods and the hurried and jarring noise of the highway. Late-model cars jockeyed for position as they sped and weaved through traffic on their way to 'wherever'.

My mind had looked just like this rush hour traffic in the middle of the night. Each thought was driving its own car rapidly down the highway. Too many thoughts traveling in too many directions. Instead of anticipating the light of a dawning day, I only focused on my stupid and controlling to-do list.

Perhaps learning to receive the new day with a spirit of anticipation and gratitude will help align my life to reflect the joy of the woods more than the chaos of the highway. Moment by moment. Step by step. Day after day. Maybe, just maybe, I'll learn to receive daily moments as well as the autumn woods.

UNFAMILIAR PATHS

Slowly it was dawning on me. Again, I was sitting in a magical place tucked under a canopy of black walnut limbs. Tiny yellow leaves fluttered down from this massive tree that's seen more than 200 autumns. And I was the only one to witness the sight of this majestic tree preparing for winter.

I'd just spent ten minutes sweeping away two weeks' worth of this tree's debris from the deck. But this morning, sweeping wasn't a chore. The rhythmic swishing and scraping of the bristles on the deck was soothing as I gazed at the beauty around me.

The woods sat poised on the brink of fall. Squirrels chattered while claiming their storage bins in the trees. The leaves were trading their clothing of green to new outfits displaying hints of gold and burgundy and yellow. The birds sang sweetly and peacefully. Their ruthless days of fighting and territory claiming for 'nesting' rights were behind them because their young were grown and had left the nests. Chewed up walnuts and acorns dotted the ground. The background hum of the locusts welcomed this fall morning,

The fall is here. For the first time in years, the changes represented by this season squeezed gratitude up to the surface of my heart.

Because much of my life feels unknown, the predictability of seasons now brings me great comfort. I know that all the leaves

123

will eventually fall. The right birds will migrate. The autumn woods will succumb to winter. It is God's plan.

Boy oh boy do I love this predictable order of things.

Later that day, Ron, Debralyn, Josh, and I drove to Iowa to watch Jordan's college football team play. We knew he wouldn't play much, and we knew this game would be a blow-out. We also knew that at best we'd get a quick hug and brief conversation with him before we had to head back home. Without him.

But, no matter. We went to the game. Nobody could have prepared me for the joy that would exist by simply seeing each of my family's faces one after the other. The start of the game was delayed by two hours which gave us an unexpected chunk of time to sit under an autumn tree and talk. What a gift!

Jordan also got to hear us cheer. We arrived well equipped with a megaphone, cowbell, and stainless- steel water bottle to bang on metal seats. We caught his eyes several times during the game and knew his thoughts. And he knew ours. But the gifts of this day didn't end at the football game.

We drove back to our get-away house via the scenic route that night. Grayish lights reflected off the Mississippi River. A mysterious harvest moon flirted behind ever so wispy clouds. Mist wafted through the valleys. Magical and surreal. The beauty of exploring an unfamiliar road.

Contrast the breathtaking views of the unfamiliar road with the comfort of that very morning's familiar black walnut tree.

Gratitude in the unfamiliar and the familiar. This mirrors my new reality. It felt right to be thankful for both experiences.

I saw this truth a few years later in my dad. He continues to embrace the seasons even though he no longer is able to head to the field to harvest corn and soybeans. An unfamiliar road for sure.

A road that he'd hoped he would never find himself on.

It was one thing to hear Dad express gratitude when his barnyard was filled with cattle and his fields were filled with corn stalks waving in the summer breeze. When his hands were dirty with honest labor and a long day ended with a root beer float sitting in his favorite recliner. When he could walk anywhere and list anything.

It was a more powerful thing to hear my dad express gratitude when my sister and I pulled the covers over him as he began a night in a strange bed in a place he never wanted to sleep. A battle with sepsis at age 95 took a toll on his strength, and he'd found himself in a nursing home for rehabilitation.

For a man independently rooted on the farm, not being in his home was devastating. Hearing the unfamiliar voices of those who want to help him was almost impossible even with the strongest of hearing aids. He wondered when he would get home again. If he would get home again. He wondered what happened to him. His questions swirled out of control, and for the first time in my life, fear shown through his deep brown eyes. He placed his head on the strange pillow while his mind raced. The more his body tensed, the sadder my heart became.

Then came a moment when the familiar was invited into this unfamiliar road.

My sister locked her eyes with Dad's eyes as she stood at the foot of his nursing home bed. She slowly and loudly began to recite the table prayer that had been the prelude to most meals we ate as a family on the farm. With red, teary eyes and a strong voice, my dad joined her. Word by word, truth walked into this tiny, strange nursing home room. He calmed. He smiled weakly. He began to recite it once again.

"Give thanks unto the Lord for He is good. His mercies endure forever and ever. Amen."

Yes, it is one thing to hear my dad proclaim that God is good when life is good. It is quite another thing to hear my dad proclaim that God is good when life is hard. All those years of storing up what he sowed came back to calm him on his unfamiliar road.

SLOW IT DOWN

What a relief it must have been for my dad and my uncles to unload their last wagonfuls of corn into their corn cribs. They were done for another year. After missing weeks of cozy family suppers and evenings reading the newspaper, they had faithfully seized every opportunity the weather allowed to bring their harvest home.

It was time to celebrate!

When my extended family outgrew the spaces any home could accommodate, we began celebrating Thanksgiving in a forest preserve pavilion right down the road from my grandparent's farm. Practically all of my relatives farmed or at least had grown up on the farm and this was the day to shine. Table after table was filled with the goodness of the harvest. Turkeys. Stuffing. Mashed potatoes. Sweet corn from the field. Homemade rolls and fresh butter. Cream from the cow. Blue ribbon quality homemade pies.

We piled around picnic tables with overflowing paper plates commenting on who made what this year. Who grew what this year? Who overcame what this year? Even if someone had really struggled through illness or death or other significant loss in the past year, collectively we still celebrated Thanksgiving.

Abundance. Gratitude. Literally from the nearby fields onto our plastic forks.

Roots of aunts and uncles and cousins formed an important part of my rural childhood. Treasuring those extended family roots

127

sitting beside me during those Thanksgiving meals continue to nourish the roots of my life today.

Few people demonstrated how to nourish relational roots more than Susan. I call her my 'fists in the air' friend because she cheers for me no matter what. I loved having her live twenty minutes away from me, and we'd committed to running through life together.

Foolishly I'd expected to do that as 'neighbors.' When she told me she was moving to a new time zone, something appeared out of nowhere and kicked me in my gut. Why did my friends always seem to leave me? This one hurt so much. But it was going to happen, so I decided to say good-bye well. She beat me to the punch.

With our six kiddos under the age of ten, I offered to help her pack. With tears in my eyes, I wrapped her life up in newspapers and put it in plain brown boxes. After we piled some boxes into a corner, she whispered, "Come here. Let's go out to my van. I've got something you've got to hear."

Wearing a smile on our faces, we climbed into the back of her brown minivan. The van that had parked itself in my driveway so many times and had joined my own van on adventures to the zoo or the park or the city. Perhaps we should have worried about our six little kiddos, but we weren't.

She loaded a cassette into her van's radio and forwarded it to just the right spot. She was almost giddy with delight.

"Listen to this! You won't believe how beautifully high her voice will go. It will take your breath away!" Susan held her breath. "Wait for the magic. It's coming!"

She squeezed my dirty and tired hands with her own. We locked eyes. We listened to that magical music.

Time stood still.

Soon after our minivan mini-concert, Susan moved to another time zone. And she has lived in two more since then. To this day, nearly twenty years later, when I miss her, I find myself playing or repeat the magical minivan song. I still see her blue eyes glimmer with delight as she created that moment during so much chaos.

She slowed down the tasks of packing and moving and goodbyes long enough for me to feel what I needed to feel.

But perhaps the culmination of all that I was learning to embrace about the real me happened on 10/10/10 - October 10th, 2010.

For this woman who has strong connections to certain numbers more than others, 10/10/10 was a lobbed pitch down the center of the plate for me to knock out of the ballpark.

"Josh, did you realize that this year, we will have a 10/10/10? And that this year the Bryants have someone turning 80, 70, 50, 40, 30 and 10? And we have wedding anniversaries that will mark 30 and 20 and 10 years? Isn't that crazy?"

It could have ended right there as Josh and I drove down some road going to who remembers where. But thankfully Josh caught the significance of what I was processing aloud.

"Mom, we should have a Bryant family party on 10/10/10 starting at 10:10. We should celebrate!"

Instantly I agreed. Absolutely!!

It turned out to be one of the most special days planted right in the middle of my garden.

Who else has a family that has so many different 'decade' birthdays and anniversaries ending in a zero?

We needed, no I needed, to mark it. We needed to slow time down.

So out went the invitations.

"Come wearing clothes from the decade of your birth. Be ready to listen to music and remember trivia from your era. It's time to celebrate! We have much to be thankful for."

Simple rules.

If you were born in the 50s, dress like it.

If you were born in the 30s, dress like it.

If you were born in the 90s, dress like it.

And so on.

In other words, let's have fun celebrating, rather than calculating, the years between us.

What would it look like to slow it down enough to realize we may have more in common than we thought?

So, decades walked into my garden couple by couple. My in-laws took it far more seriously than I ever imagined. Imagine polyester leisure suits. Mod flower power hippy beads. Crazy hairstyles by men and women. Short shorts for guys wearing tube socks.

A vivid feast across time for the eyes.

The fun and playfulness in the air was palpable. Embracing the decade of our birth leveled the playing field. We weren't taking ourselves too seriously, and the laughter was so good for our souls.

But there was a moment that still takes my breath away.

Everyone who stood in our backyard that day can still see my father-in-law and mother-in-law round the corner into garden sporting their own decade's outfits. Delight mischievously written on their faces lit up our backyard.

Grandchildren burst into laughter as they saw their gangster grandpa and their movie star grandma join the party. They fully engaged in the vision that Josh and I had to celebrate all the decades of life given to our family.

We recently had to say goodbye to the man who, alongside his wife, created this whole group of Bryants. Any of us would give just about anything to see this man, this husband, this dad, and this grandpa round the corner into the garden with a huge smile on his face. With huge hugs ready to give. But we will have to wait until the other side of this life. Earthly good-byes make no sense at all.

Why do I still look at that spot in my garden wishing I could see him walk around the corner?

Maybe the better question is why is that moment so vivid? What was it about that moment that slowed it all down for me? Was it that the hurried agendas of life got left behind that day? Was it because we soaked in moments like nothing else in the world mattered that day?

Maybe.

Fast forward to Fall 2016. Chicago Cubs. World Series Champions.

Oh.My.Goodness.

I'd been a loyal, yet pessimistic Chicago Cubs fan since 1969.

Every spring, it was exactly the same. Maybe this would be the year.

Every fall, it was exactly the same. Maybe next year.

Until 2016. I couldn't help but hold my breath with every, literally every, pitch as my Cubbies survived games and series.

And then it was game seven of the World Series! I could not take a deep breath.

Would this be the year?

Their coach, Joe Madden, had drilled this simple phrase into his players' minds as the season of miracles progressed into the playoffs.

You've guessed it.

"Slow it down."

Here was his logic. The adrenaline rush of pressure-packed baseball games makes everything louder and faster. Wisely, Madden didn't want his Chicago Cubs to miss the joy of this miraculous experience by worrying about their next at-bat or their next pitch. Or their next game.

It almost seemed that it mattered more to Madden that his team noticed the joy of this miraculous season rather than winning the game.

So, slow it down. Feel the moment. Feel the intensity, excitement, or even fear of the moment.

But slow it down enough to feel it.

You won't be able to feel it unless you slow it down.

That's what gathering in a forest preserve did on Thanksgiving.

That's what Susan did in her minivan.

That's what happened as we celebrated the decades in my backyard garden.

And that's why I couldn't stop jumping up and down in my living room when the Cubs won the World Series. I had slowed it all down to soak it all in.

VAULT FRIENDS

I've lived in the comfort zone of embracing the familiar rather than jumping into the excitement of embracing something new.

For example, I don't have a favorite season except the one that I'm in. Forgive me for digressing in a book about fall, but if it was spring outside, I'd be all about the lilacs, tulips, dandelions, and rain showers. And I can't understand how people watch the magic of snow falling while complaining it's not summer.

I'll admit it takes me a while to embrace drooping tulips, closing swimming pools, migrating birds, and melting snow. Transitions, even those within the natural rhythm of the four seasons, are hard. Probably because those changes are outside of my control.

Even though I'm learning to embrace what's new and next in my life, I still lean into soaking up the familiar whenever I can.

Imagine my delight when I got an email from a woman that I have known since fourth grade. Her familiar 'voice' stretched through time and touched me.

"Are you free for lunch with all of us?" Robin asked. I immediately saw the faces that composed "all of us." I couldn't remember the last time that we'd been together.

I'd been friends with Marian since before first grade. I met Robin and Diana when my tiny school consolidated with their only slightly larger grade school. Four more girls, Noreen, Chris, Pam, and Teresa joined us as freshmen from the remaining nooks and crannies of the rural communities that fed students into Newark High School.

It wasn't an easy thing for a group of eight girls to figure out relationships while we were still trying to figure out our own place in life. But we chose to giggle more than argue. We chose to cheer for one another rather than compete. Throughout the week, we pursued our classes, after-school activities, and boys. But we always found our way back to each other. After all, we knew each other. We knew all our parents, siblings, the color of our bedrooms, and the names of our pets. Secrets, dreams, frustrations, and fears were all safe with us.

Without realizing it, we were planting the value of knowing exactly what it felt like to grow up in our small town together.

When our group of eight became a very, very sad group of seven, we huddled up a little more closely. None of us knew how to really talk about losing Chris, but we all knew that we really wanted to have her back. That painful good-bye broke through our self-centered senioritis. Life was fragile. And hard. And confusing.

But it was our senior year after all. It was time to take the ACTs, apply to colleges, find prom dresses, perform our senior play, and create our final yearbook. While we never spoke of it, my hunch is that we all wondered what life outside of our little safe and comfy group was going to feel like.

Seven of us hugged each other before we marched down the aisle and across the stage to receive our diploma in late May of 1978. Tears and promises to stay in touch.

After all, no one who had not grown up in our little town could know anything about it. We would always be there for each other.

You know where this is heading, right?

Different colleges. Some new boyfriends. Weddings. Babies. Careers. New homes in different zip codes. Losing parents and siblings.

Even though I had promised to not lose touch, I had. I wasn't the only one.

I'd heard through my small-town grapevine sources that Marian was sick. Like really, really sick. I'd known Marian since I was four, and I don't have a single school class picture or important school memory without her in it. My memories of and affection for her stirred me deeply.

Marian's illness was the last straw in Robin's mind. Far too much time had passed without us once again sitting around a table getting into everyone's business. In a good and familiar way of course.

Trying to describe our first reconnection as a group of seven adult women is like trying to describe a winter sunset without using adjectives.

But one of my richest gifts in this season of fall was saying yes to that email invitation. Robin, brave and honest and smart, had the guts to tackle the gathering of this cluster of cats.

So, we all showed up at her house, plopped down on her kitchen chairs, and didn't budge for the next seven hours. We had three decades to make up for after all.

At this first precious reunion, we started by asking and answering the 'facts' of life.

How old is your son? What does your husband do? Have you heard from so and so? Wait, who is so and so? What's it like to be a mother-in-law? And so on and so forth.

Whenever there was even the slightest pause in our conversation, someone shared a story from grade or high school that caused us to slide back in time. We laughed until our sides hurt as we traveled back and forth between then and now. I kept waiting to wake up from this dream! I had no idea how much I had needed to reconnect with my familiar relational roots. But here it was, and I wasn't going to miss a second or a word of it.

Most of us had lost at least one parent since high school graduation, and we couldn't believe how comforting it was to be with people who knew our roots. They knew I loved the Cubs, now, and peanut M&Ms. They remembered my hurt at not being asked to the junior prom. They also had not forgotten that I had to

135

get dropped off first after our escapades because I was the only one who had a curfew.

None of my girlfriends that I do life with now knew my mom, and they didn't grow up in Newark. I'd been longing for something I hadn't known was missing.

The roots we share of our 'formative' years felt like family. All of us are in the thick of changes. Empty nest. Teenage driver. Sick parents. Health struggles. Grandbabies. Kids in college. Post-childrearing careers.

Boy did it feel good to be around the familiar in the middle of all that. We all drew a special strength and comfort from our collective connections.

Marian's health continued to decline. We needed to all be together with her as she was dying, and she wanted us to make sure that we didn't stop.

And we haven't even though our number is down to six. Even after Marian's death, her intensely unique personality lingers in the air, and we all feel it when we're together. All we have to do is say, "Ah, that's Marian...." With a flick of that childhood hand that only we see, we see. Yes. Marian. We see you.

It's already been nearly a decade since I opened Robin's email. We have continued to nurture our growing friendships and don't need to rely on memories when we sit around tables in our homes or in restaurants. We are more likely to start with current concerns or celebrations while resting on the comfort of history. And our group texts come with honesty and regularity.

While I don't even remember what the issue was, I do remember how I prefaced a conversation one afternoon sitting at Pam's dining room table.

"Please don't tell anyone about this."

To which Pam immediately replied, "Who am I going to tell? None of my friends around here know you! It's going in the vault."

She was right! Who are we going to tell?

At that moment, we decided to call ourselves the "vault friends". We can be safe and honest and real. We do that much better as adults than we did as teens, but that foundation of knowing and familiar means so much more because of all the years we have for context.

So, armed with the internet and cell phones, we alert each other to celebrations and struggles. Often before we have told others. We'd drop everything to find ways to show up for each other. Kind of like family would.

Earlier this fall, Robin got married and her 'vault' girls were there front and center to cheer and dance and celebrate her joy! But we didn't just show up because we went to school together eons ago. We showed up because our relationships matter. They're growing. They're real.

So, we danced together at her wedding reception just like we danced in our high school gymnasium. Yet somehow this felt more precious.

We've embraced the beauty of our vault friend dance steps that no one who had not grown up with us could know anything about.

YOU GOT THIS

I've worked hard to silence the fearful spirit that had taken root in my heart whenever I thought I might fail. I'd realized that tackling a challenge, even if I failed or needed to ask for help, should go in the win column.

I've been able to recognize my mom's words of encouragement during my youth were only meant to encourage me. If I'd ask her to elaborate, I can almost hear her encourage my freedom to try new things without any pressure of succeeding.

It felt so good to say yes or no to opportunities without letting fear of failure be my guiding principle. The fear filter was fading.

When my friend asked me to alter her daughter's bridesmaid's dress, I was eager to help.

Weeks later, the disassembled pale pink bridesmaid's dress lay in four pieces covering my kitchen table. These weren't simple pieces either. Each of them had layers of chiffon covering satin. I knew that I dare not make a mistake putting it all back together. I kept telling myself to be careful with my scissors. Why had my friend told me that the dress had cost $300?

How quickly that old fear of failure and self-doubt seeped in. It had seemed quite simple when I told my friend's daughter that I could make it fit and save her the $100 alteration fee. Boy did I hope this wasn't an impulsive and costly 'oops'.

My kitchen was quiet, and I was finally in the mood to tackle this project. Just keep ripping, marking, and measuring. What had that once completed dress looked like? The one-piece that was now four? Once the zipper was dangling, I began to really get nervous. I wish I'd taken a picture of it. I guess I could fork over the $100 to a tailor if worse came to worse.

Then Debralyn danced through the kitchen on her way to the basement with two of her friends. Intuitively she saw the strained look on my face. She's always been able to read my body language like I'm a large-type book.

Her chipper voice shattered the silence. "How's it going, Mom?"

"Well, I really hope I can put this all back together."

"Mom. There's nobody else I'd trust more to fix a dress. You got this." And off she went to study statistics with her friends.

Once again, the kitchen quieted. I turned my attention back to the dress while replaying her words of confidence in my mind. She had reminded me of what was true. I could alter this dress. I'd been altering or making wedding dresses since I was twelve. I began to slowly put this dress back together piece by piece by piece.

Debralyn simply smiled when she saw the former pile of pale pink fabric now hanging in one piece over the back of the door. I don't think I could have done it without her.

I had no idea if I would be able to alter that dress when I said yes, but it was a powerful taste of how great it feels to take a risk. And even though it worked out this time, I would have been ok if I had needed to ask or even pay for help. Taking the risk was what mattered.

The very next day found Debralyn and me heading to Great America. While some moms and daughters spend the day shopping or getting mani/pedis, we prefer amusement parks. We head toward the front row of every roller coaster and stand face to face as we wait in the long lines. Our conversations never falter, and we almost lose our voices from giggling while we fly through the air.

This time, however, Debralyn began to dig around a seed she'd planted a couple of weeks earlier.

"Mom. You'd love it. It's like skydiving. You gotta try it. I know you'd love it."

Note. I'd never said I wanted to go skydiving.

I think I mumbled something very noncommittal in return. But she'd succeeded in making me think about it.

Dare Devil Dive.

I'm not sure how high in the air you rise before you free fall directly toward the concrete, but it is, in fact, the tallest structure in the entire amusement park. I kind of remembered that the speed of the free fall would warrant a traffic ticket on most expressways.

As we wound our way around the circumference of the park riding everything in our path, she said, 'Let's do it now Mom. You got this.'"

I don't quite remember what I said, but she heard "OK!" And she grabbed my arm and off we went.

At this moment, our roles reversed. She'd been on this ride before, so she talked me through every detail.

Her description of the harness details, the slow float to the top, and the reality that I will feel nothing is securely holding me as I plummet to the ground all began to blur in my mind. I'm the mom. Isn't she supposed to be leaning on me?

So, we got strapped in, then we were placed in a cranelike structure. All the while I was joking around with the employees trying not to look up to where we were headed.

"Fly time!" I tried to make my voice sound brave.

Up, indeed, we went. And up we continued to go. I think I said a lot of things to my dear daughter during our ascent, but I honestly have little memory of it. I kept thinking that I clearly hadn't thought this through. When the people beneath us began to look like grasshoppers, Debralyn said, "Look around Mom. Isn't it amazing?"

That normally would be something I would say. I took a quick and stiff glance around me, nodded, and then kept my eyes focused on the ground. I didn't think I agreed with her.

Then the ride operator shouted out to 'Jes' to be ready to pull the ripcord. For some reason, Debralyn had chosen the name 'Jes' for this ride.

One. Two. Three.

Then my daughter pulled the ripcord.

I didn't stop screaming until the flight ended. I have little memory of any thoughts other than I didn't want to let go of Debralyn's arm.

When we finally stood on terra firma again, it took about an hour for my brain and heart to settle down. Processing what had just happened, I realized I was overwhelmed with how much comfort I took in being linked with Debralyn. I couldn't have imagined doing it all alone. The rush of the fall required that I needed to be connected tightly to someone.

Later it hit me just like the wind had hit my face on our free fall. Two days in a row I leaned on my daughter. Her words about the dress. Her arm linked in mine during flight. And I really loved how that felt. It was ok to lean on her.

In what felt like just a few more blinks of my eyes, Debralyn was in her senior year of college, engaged to Marc, and planning their wedding. This daughter of mine who had curled up in the same position on the burgundy leather sofa for most of her life. Comfy blankets tossed over her even comfier sweatpants. Her profile still familiar, but now looking like a woman.

Whenever she was at home sitting in that spot, I stared at her from my corner of the room. Whether she knew I was staring or not, she didn't let on.

I'm going to really miss her. I'm really going to miss the way it has always been.

No matter how much I celebrate the woman that she has become, no matter how much I celebrate God's direction in her life, and no matter how much I know that I have to let her go, I still know that I'm going to miss her.

So, holding both emotions in my heart, I leaned in with joyful enthusiasm to help plan her wedding.

And it was fun. So many times, I wanted to pinch myself that we actually were growing closer as we planned and strategized and created. Not many fathers enter the planning of a wedding like Ron did and that also created moment after moment of rich connection.

Probably the main character of all this wedding planning turned out to be her wedding dress. I definitely didn't want to be the one to choose the dress, but I definitely longed for a special moment in all of her dress hunting ventures.

Before we left for the bridal salon appointment, I asked her what she needed from me.

"Oh Mom, you know me. You'll know what I need." I sure hope so. Was this code for her reminding me again that I've got this? So many things in this season that I've never done before, but I was getting used to that feeling.

So, armed with bridesmaids in tow, we headed to the bridal salon and obediently sat outside of the dressing room waiting for her to appear wearing dress number one. The mirror-lined stage was poised for her to twirl and smile. I couldn't help but see little seven-year-old Debralyn pretending to be a bride with a white dress-up gown.

She loved the first dress she tried on. It was exactly what she had predicted she would wear on her wedding day. Number two didn't last long. And then she tried on number three.

I knew it was her favorite before she did when she declared, "I'm so confused."

In Debralyn style, she solicited all her attendants' opinions and much to her dismay, their decision wasn't unanimous. I tried to

143

stay small and quiet in my chair because I knew it was only a matter of time before I'd get the big question. As I tried to gather my input, I listened again to the words she'd spoken before we left home that day.

"Mom, you know me. You'll know what I need."

So, when she asked me which dress I liked best, I joined her on the mirror-lined platform and asked her to look me in my eyes while I tenderly took her hands in mine.

I told her that she'd already made the most important decision by saying 'yes' to Marc when he proposed. Then I asked if the way she felt in this dress matched how she wanted to feel when she said "I do" to Marc on their wedding day. The tears that flowed from her eyes were her answer.

That's when I knew I had my moment with my daughter. It felt so good to have learned how to slow it down and lean into holding all the emotions at once.

Months later, dress number three gave me a bonus moment with Debralyn on her wedding day. I'd not orchestrated it or even longed for it. But when it became available, even on one of the busiest days of my life, I was able to seize it. Here's how it unfolded.

After a few hours of hair and make-up and eating and hydrating, surrounded by her bridesmaids, Debralyn put on her wedding dress. Dress number three. It was about time to officially join her life with Marc's.

As she stood in our living room, her joy took my breath away. And then it hit me. I wanted, no I needed, to be the one to weave the satin ribbons through the countless loops down the back of her dress. That was the last 'thing' that needed to be done before she'd get in the car with Ron to head off for her 'first look' with Marc.

I'd grown so familiar with the back of her dress that summer because I figured out how to bustle it. But the dress had been empty then. This day it held my precious Debralyn.

There were so many people wandering around my house and my front yard. And my kitchen was a mess. But none of that mattered. All I could see was Debralyn standing in front of our couch wearing her dress that she wanted to wear when she said "I do" to Marc. I was not going to miss this special touch.

With tears in my eyes and with trembling fingers, I wove and wove those white satin ribbons through every loop down the back of her dress. And when I finished, I whispered something special in her ear.

"You got this." And so do I.

BLUE SKIES

What began as a 'business' agreement to teach piano to Debralyn and Josh turned into a deep connection between Marilyn and me.

Wednesdays. 9 am. A place for this busy homeschool mom to exhale and listen to the beautiful music Marilyn helped them create. Without realizing it, this little space on the corner of her floral couch in her living room began to fill a 'mom-shaped' hole in my heart.

She flitted around the room like a bumblebee doing all she could to help my children 'feel' the music. Colorful scarves waved to demonstrate flow, balls bounced to capture rhythm, and feet danced to create freedom and delight. I'd never seen such a dedicated and creative teacher. But I had also never seen a woman who could open her heart to so many people and welcome them inside.

Lessons never began at the piano. Lessons began with Marilyn pausing long enough to check in with 'mother'. She wanted to know what I was teaching the kids. What I was knitting. What I was making for supper. What I loved about growing up on a farm. What I was going to do on April Fool's Day. What those tears in my eyes meant.

She seemed to be able to read the nuances of my life like she could read the nuances of a piece of music.

So, each week, Wednesdays at 9, I showed up. The errands that needed to be run during lessons always waited. Why on earth would I miss a chance to 'be' in her presence?

Years passed. We marked the seasons together by noticing the autumn breeze as she stood at the door waving good-bye. She entered my joy anytime a snowstorm was on the horizon. We marveled at the perfect peony bloom that she placed on her coffee table.

More importantly, she asked me how I was handling the transitions in our family. As child after child headed off to college or fell in love, she anticipated the song my heart was playing and knew exactly how to encourage me. She empathized without telling me how to feel. She had this uncanny ability to paint a picture of future beauty without discounting whatever I felt that day.

I never left her home without her reminder to 'make it a great day'.

And then I became her student. Trading the floral couch for her piano bench made me feel vulnerable and small at first.

Yet, finding the courage to take piano lessons was one of the wisest decisions I made as I was learning how to be healthy and embrace the changes of fall in my life. It was a brave step into being me again, and Marilyn was a significant voice in my journey.

Later she infused me with confidence and with her hands literally resting upon mine as I played, music began to capture my heart again. Even after my children ended their lessons, I kept showing up with eagerness. You see, we had also become friends.

It was during one of my private lessons that she invited me to enter into her new reality.

Aphasia. A cruel disease that was taking away her ability to find her words. My hands began to tremble, and my tears began to flow.

She took my face in her hands and turned it to gaze out her window.

"Look at that magnificent sky. Isn't it the most beautiful color of blue? The sky will be the blue sky whether I can say the word or not. Isn't that amazing? I have so much to be happy about!" Marilyn was not making any of her optimism up. That's how she had chosen to live her life.

She bravely and enthusiastically jumped into the world of memory care. This brilliant, wise, adventurous woman was doing all she could do to keep exercising her mind. It wasn't beneath her. She viewed this as something else for her to learn.

She could have chosen bitterness. She chose gratitude. She lived out her encouragement to 'make it a great day.'

Marilyn always loved to play duets with her students at the end of their lessons, and I was no exception.

Aphasia finally forced her to stop teaching, but I still stopped in to see her from time to time. During one of my last visits, she practically danced her way to the piano telling me we must make time for a duet before I left. I'm so glad that I chose to be late for my next appointment because that turned out to be the last time we played together. She pulled out a simple copy of "Let there be Peace on Earth."

This was the first time that I had to 'wait' for her as we played. The tears flowed down my face as we created our music because the moment felt so tender. I was looking for something profound to say when we finished, but of course, she beat me to it.

"We've got to take this on the road, you know."

Yep. That's what she always said.

I've heard it said that what's inside of a person comes out more clearly as they age. What was inside of her was delight and affection.

When I saw Marilyn for the last time, she no longer could find my name. But, no matter. She let me into her heart through her crystal blue eyes that still danced with delight. They knew me. They looked at every picture of my children and grandchildren that I could show her.

She mustered up the phrase, "I've got so much. I'm so happy." She was telling the truth. She gave and received love so generously. What more could a person need?

I didn't want to leave her that day. And the truth was that we had no song to play together. But I still stepped into her living room and looked at the floral couch and piano bench where I had learned so much more than how to play music.

Then I stood at the bottom of her stairs while she climbed up three so she could reach my face to give me a good-bye kiss.

She's always been up ahead of me. And she's always reached out to give me what I need. Even then. And even now.

The fall sky on the day of her funeral was the most beautiful color blue. The brilliant red and orange leaves of the majestic maple trees couldn't even compete with the saturated blue of the sky. I could hear her reminder that the sky was still blue whether she could find the words or not. I smiled that on the day I would say my final earthly goodbye to my friend, she was still teaching me.

I had lunch with her daughter, Lisa, a few months later. I was curious how this woman who loved life so deeply handled its end.

I shouldn't have been surprised by the beautiful picture Lisa painted.

Marilyn had continued to smile and dance to music around her home. Even after her aphasia worsened and more physical difficulties arose, she held onto her optimistic spirit. But she was disappearing bit by bit while trips to and from the emergency room were increasing.

Eventually, she found herself in a memory care unit where Lisa discovered her sitting in a wheelchair making beautiful, gentle archlike movements with her arms. As the music played, Marilyn reached out to take a woman's hand to bounce along with the rhythm of the song. Even as her life was slipping away, she was holding onto and inviting another to notice what was happening.

In her wheelchair, she was dancing. She was making it a great day.

"When He calls me, I'm going to Him," Marilyn said multiple times with passion and urgency.

And she did. When she slipped into a coma, she clearly was at peace and pain-free. A harpist came into her room about an hour before she died. He played music to her breathing. And her breathing seemed to join the rhythmic dance of the music.

Is it possible that after dancing joyfully throughout her life, she was now dancing her way into eternity?

This spritely woman who once wore sassy glasses and always had a hot cup of coffee at the ready. Who rarely wore the same outfit twice and loved decorating her home for Christmas. Who knew how to make even the simplest song sound like magic.

Who taught me to look at the sky and pick peonies and celebrate the tiniest of moments.

"Look at that sky, Marilyn. It's the perfect blue for the fall leaves. You've got all your words now. I'll keep looking at the sky. And I'll choose to make it a great day."

DANCING FEET

I used to hide in the trunk of Marian's car or behind the gymnasium staircase when it was time to run laps during high school gym class. Eventually, I overcame my aversion to all things running and transformed into someone who enjoyed a regular three-mile run through my suburban neighborhoods.

A strange longing began to surface whenever I heard the word marathon. I quickly silenced it. Me? Run a marathon? I think not. My longest run at that point may have been about six miles.

But the longing only got louder. Would this be a way to silence my fear of failure once and for all? Timidly I began to increase my mileage and eventually began to train for the Chicago Marathon. I fell in love with the challenge and discipline of following a strategy that seemed like it could possibly work.

All through the hot and humid summer days, I ran up and down the running path and along my neighborhood streets. The cooler fall temperatures signaled that race day was approaching. Finally.

Two weeks before the targeted race day while I was finishing my final long training run, I had an unforgettable experience. Even before the actual race, I had a hunch that my longing had been an invitation into that specific moment.

It went something like this.

My heart was overwhelmed with gratitude for the opportunity I'd just had to train for this marathon. I began silently pouring out my thankfulness to God. I was amazed that He had helped orchestrate my training runs, kept my body relatively healthy, and helped me avoid any injuries. My long runs had never battled a rainstorm. The sheer beauty on my routes came from His hand. I went on and on as my feet kept running toward home.

Suddenly my spirit sensed His response. I actually looked toward the sky because His presence felt so strong. Could it be? Did I hear Him right?

He seemed to be impressing on me that it was His pleasure to watch me do this. His joy mirrored mine.

What?

Yes, it's true. I sensed God delighting in my delight. Not in my accomplishments or efforts, but in my delight. In my joy. And I hadn't even run the race yet. He experienced delight?

I was doing something that He had put in my heart to do. I was living out a part of Linda that He had created. And He had joy? I intuitively knew that this wasn't the only part of my life that He danced over with joy.

Well, that changes everything. It shouldn't have surprised me as much as it did as I thought about it over the years.

That's because I was a mom. I took delight in what delighted each of my three children from practically the day they were born. Why in the world had I not transferred that to how God delighted over me?

By the time he was one week old, Jordan loved a tiny fuzzy yellow chick that made a goofy squeaking noise when we shook it. Once Debralyn discovered her little white blanket with satin trim, she rarely let it go. And Josh was so partial to my satin and terrycloth robe that it usually replaced his own blanket. From the earliest of days, I saw what delighted my children.

And over the years it continued. Jordan began to ride his bicycle without training wheels. Debralyn read any book that I gave her even though I don't remember teaching her how to read. Josh created music out of almost nothing regardless of the instrument he was playing.

Their delight continued to bring me delight.

In the little and in the big moments. In every season as they grew.

As Ron and I were raising them, we had tried to intentionally create a home where our three children could create strong and deep roots. That was the easy part.

Growing roots to give them the courage to take flight with strong and well-developed wings made things a bit more emotional.

My heart was wrecked when I heard a song on the radio one day. Once the lyrics began to sink in, I had to pull my car over to the side of the road because my tears were blinding me. Here was our parenting vision flowing out of my car's speakers.

Pay attention to your roots. Nourish them. Know them. Embrace them.

Grow roots dear children. Then we all will celebrate your wings. Delight in the roots and delight in the wings. Thank you, Mark Harris, for your lyrics in *Find Your Wings*.

If I'm honest, I'm more a fan of roots. That's selfish yes. Wings include leaving, and changes create ripples. Yet learning how to say good-bye to the way things were and embracing the new reality has been covered in the image of roots and wings.

People commonly ask how I handled the rapid changes in our family. Weddings, college, moving out, yadda, yadda, yadda. After learning how to hold more than one emotion at a time, I've resisted the 'expected' response.

You know how that sounds.

"Oh, this is a wonderful opportunity for (insert name of child). I am so excited for (insert name of same child). I can't wait to see what happens for (insert once again name of child)."

155

Instead of stopping with the above, I add the following.

"Yes, I feel delighted for (insert name of child), but I also feel this."

This is when I put my right hand slightly above my stomach and say that this is the part of me that aches when I have to say good-bye to the way things were. Longing. Hurting. Missing.

Even if we say we are honored and proud and blessed to watch our brave, young children attack the world. Even if we are 100% convinced this is the way it is supposed to be.

Even if we must grieve for a little bit.

Who am I? I had started this journey numbing anything that felt uncomfortable. And now I am comfortable saying that letting go is hard?

Yes. Because only then can I embrace joy. The time to hold on had ended. The time to dance had come.

Yes, I had some dancing to do. Actually, I've had lots of dancing to do.

At Jordan and Jacqui's wedding, my eyes filled with tears when Jacqui danced with her dad. I'd just told her dad that we had tried to raise a good man to be his precious daughter's husband. I felt his deep longing to find his little girl again. But we both knew that season was over. Our children were grown up and joining their lives together.

I saw Jordan standing off in the distance. And it slowly began to dawn on me. I leaned over to Ron and said, "They aren't going to play that song for Jordan and me, are they?" Speechlessly my right hand found that special spot above my stomach.

But Jordan and I marked his new marriage by dancing to the music that had captured my heart years ago. Mother and son. Literally holding on and letting go. Sowing and reaping. Roots and wings. Time stood still under a canopy of life.

Delight and tears in both of our eyes. Holding close and releasing.

Jordan knows without a doubt that his roots will hold and support him. And he also knows that his parents will be the loudest cheerleaders for him as he flies.

Fast forward six years to a different son and a different song. But the same mother's heart.

When each of our children turned thirteen, Ron and I celebrated them with a gift that honored their unique loves and wiring. Given the way Josh engaged with music, using a song, *My Wish* by Rascal Flatts, was an obvious choice.

You would think that I would have been prepared for how this would go. Because Jordan chose a special song for our mother and son dance at his wedding, I should have realized that Josh would also play a special song for our dance when he joined his life with Natasha.

But I didn't figure it out until its music began to filter across the dance floor. I tearfully joined Josh. Our youngest son. Now an adult and husband. We looked into each other's eyes and talked about the love we shared. He gently and confidently led me in circles around the dance floor. I had already watched him dance with Natasha. The give and take of their first dance was sheer beauty.

But my dancing comparisons with his new wife melted away. This was my son. We were dancing. He knew that I wished that more than anything I wanted his life to reflect the lyrics of this song.

Mother and son. Literally holding on and letting go. Sowing and reaping. Roots and wings. Time stood still under a canopy of life.

Delight and tears in both of our eyes. Holding close and releasing. Step by step.

And then it was over. When the music stopped, I looked into Josh's eyes.

Time had stopped. Both of us acknowledged that we'd forgotten anyone else was in the room. It was the most precious moment.

All three of our children had found their wings.

What began as a love story between Ron and me eventually became a family of five. Then that family grew to six. Then seven. And eight. And nine. And ten. And eleven. Each of our children married. And one of my children now had three children. Who knows what our 'final' number will be?

My precious family of eleven was gathered for the last time in our Galena home.

Ron and I had wisely decided to sell this precious piece of 'Bryant' real estate, yet we weren't quite prepared for the emotion that would surface in all of us. Sometimes the right thing to do isn't the easiest thing to do.

We'd owned this stunning piece of real estate at exactly the right time for our family. For as our family began to expand, this home was able to absorb not just the growth, but the new foundation for a new reality. We loved heading to our second home in Galena that allowed us to come together as one as well as separate into four-family units. All under the same roof.

But as time marched on, gathering in our Galena home became more challenging and more infrequent. Ron and I honestly didn't like being there alone because this had been our 'future family' home.

The time to sell, as I said, had come. And so did a buyer. It had all happened so slowly and yet so suddenly so fast.

Before I knew it, we had a signed contract and the days were dwindling when our garage opener would still let us in.

Tenderly we asked our children if they could come to Galena for a final weekend together. Yes, we had tons of work to do, but we wanted to slow it down first and just be together.

Everyone that mattered to me was there. All eleven of us. Ron. Jordan and Jacqui with their kiddos Carter, Riley, and Ashlyn. Debralyn and Marc. Josh and Natasha. I can still see us wandering up and down the staircases, sitting in the sunroom, lingering around the dining room table, and meandering into the living room.

An evening I will carry with me the rest of my life happened in that very living room. Ron set up some music to play in the background after the little ones had fallen asleep in bed. Before I knew it, the coffee table was pushed off to the side and each of us grabbed our spouse and began dancing across the wooden floor while the sun set. Four couples. Dancing. Celebrating the life that had happened under the roof in our Galena home.

Why hadn't we done this before? That answer is probably irrelevant because at least we were doing it on that night.

But it gets even better. After we sat down, our children smirked at one another and pulled out a photo of the woods that surrounded this precious home. And for the next few hours, we sat in a circle of love capturing life in words. Each of us would grab' a word that represented our family in that space, followed by the story behind it. Then we wrote the word down on our photo.

I had no idea that all the little things had grown so big in the hearts of our children. That even while I was trying to get my feet to feel stable underneath me, our kids were developing their own roots and comfort in our family.

I had no idea.

What a precious harvest of life was reaped that summer evening. I was beyond grateful.

Later that month, Ron and I handed over the keys to the new owners at closing. I was determined to be strong and steady when I met the couple that I had only seen through the eyes of our real estate negotiations.

It didn't take me long to imagine them living in our home. The home where time stood still. We were going through logistics about propane gas, garage door openers, and lawn mowing services.

I'm not quite sure how it happened, but I watched myself showing the new owner the picture that we had created that evening. All those words representing all that life. She seemed eager to hear more.

159

So cautiously I told her, with tears in my eyes, to treasure all that this home could offer. That's all I could really get out.

But what I wanted to say was to stand on the deck after dark under a moonless sky. The stars will take your breath away.

Drink coffee in the sunroom while you watch the birds dance in the trees.

Lay on the floor in the loft after the Galena parades and divide up all the candy.

Pick blackberries that you'll discover each July even if it means you end up with some prickly burrs sticking to your socks.

Notice every deer that wanders through the backyard.

Enjoy the whirlpool bath gazing at freshly fallen snow.

Linger a little. Listen more closely. Be yourself.

Ron and I didn't want to walk out of the downtown Galena attorney's office that day. We didn't want to be tourists after being part-time homeowners for two decades.

We were so sad.

I didn't know what else to do, so standing in the middle of the quiet morning street, I put my arms around Ron. My love and my rock. The man who has stood by me through every bit of my journey to becoming real.

And we began to dance

SPECIAL THANKS

My eyes were opened to the influence creation played in my life through the teaching of Nancy Beach and John Ortberg. The four seasons haven't looked the same to me since incorporating their words into my life.

My heart is overcome with gratitude to the many honest encouragers who walked alongside me during my season of change. Each of you listened to my struggles with tears in your eyes and celebrated my growth with smiles on your faces. Thank you, Susan, Lisa, Sibyl, Mindy, Angel, Brenda, Cathy, Nancy, and 'vault friends'. Your love and faithful support helped me become real.

Writing a book became more of a challenge than I'd expected. I was so grateful for the words of wisdom that lined my writing path. They came at just about the right time. To Keri, Marilyn, Jacqui, Carole, Linda, Shirley, and Naomi, thank you. You recommended tools, pointed me in the right direction, and reminded me that I needed to encourage others with my words.

But the true heroes of *Dancing in the Fall* are Ron, Jordan and Jacqui, Debralyn and Marc, and Josh and Natasha. Just as the seasons need one another, we need each other too. So often I want to pinch myself because I get to live this life loving and being loved by each of you. Words can't quite capture the love I feel for each of you, but let's just keep dancing, ok?

RESOURCES

Margery Williams, *The Velveteen Rabbit,* (New York: Alfred A. Knopf Publishers, 1985).

Annie Dillard, *Pilgrim at Tinker Creek,* (New York: HarperCollins Publishers, 1974), 16-17.

C.S. Lewis, *The Beloved Works of C.S. Lewis,* (New York: Inspirational Press), 10-11.

Mark Harris, "Find Your Wings," *The Line Between the Two,* 2005.

Rascal Flatts, "My Wish," *Me and My Gang,* 2006.

TO CONNECT

Thanks again for sharing this journey with me! It's been an honor to share my story with you.

It's my hope that you feel encouraged and inspired to embrace the truest parts of yourself as well as to keep on noticing the people and moments in your life.

While I'd love to chat with you walking through my local forest preserve or drinking a cup of coffee, I do have a few ways we can connect.

Head over to my blog at www.lindabryant.wordpress.com.

Email me at lbryantvp@gmail.com. I'd love to hear from you!

We can also connect at www.vantagepointassoc.com.

Finally, I'd love to talk to you about your upcoming event and any future speaker needs. Then we'd get to meet in person!

Again, thank you. I look forward to hearing from you.

Made in the USA
Monee, IL
06 March 2020